Homosexuality Chose Me

By

Kamia White

Studio KWest Publishing Group

Kamia White Kingdom Solutions LLC

Scripture quotations marked (TLB) are taken from The Living Bible copyright © 1971. Used by permission of Tyndale House Publishers, a Division of Tyndale House Ministries, Carol Stream, Illinois 60188. All rights reserved.

Holy Bible, New Living Translation, copyright © 1996, 2004, 2015 by Tyndale House Foundation. Used by permission of Tyndale House Publishers, Inc., Carol Stream, Illinois 60188. All rights reserved.

Scriptures marked as "(GNT)" are taken from the Good News Translation - Second Edition © 1992 by American Bible Society. Used by permission.

Studio KWest Publishing Group

A Division of Kamia White Kingdom Solutions, LLC

Printed in the United States of America

ISBNs:

ISBN: 978-0-578-62913-1 (Paperback)

Table of Content

DEDICATION

This dedication of this book is to my parents, the late Mr. and Mrs. Clinton White, and my Great Grandmother, the late Josephine Butler. Without their sacrifices, my life would not have evolved. My parents taught me valuable lessons that will be with me forever. Their unconditional love for me during my failures gave me the strength to overcome suicide. The helped me rewrite my story and celebrate my victories.

My Great Grandmother, Josephine Butler, departed her life before I was born. Hearing stories about her leadership and prayer life in her community revealed the call upon my life. Many came to Christ on her porch as she conducted prayer services. She was very influential in helping to establish the First Born Church of The Living God, Inc. It's an honor to continue her legacy in ministry.

ACKNOWLEDGMENTS

First, I thank God for the precious privilege of having another chance to share His incredible love for the lost. He has restored my soul and blessed me tremendously, and for that, I am humbled and grateful.

To my Father in the Lord, Bishop Enoch, your unfailing love throughout my life is unexplainable. Your sacrifice enabled me to dedicate my life again to my first love, Jesus Christ.

I'd also like to thank my leaders Pastor Tramesa, Pastor Jared, Pastor Audrey, Pastor Regina, and my "Reviving Souls Family" for working so diligently behind the scenes. You covered all bases helping to fulfill the vision of this project. Your heart to believe that we were moving as God revealed the plans for us, was a leap of faith. To my media and glam squad, Tammie, thank you. To my ministry friend, Melissa, you've been a great supporter from the first time you encountered God's Presence at Reviving Souls, thank you.

I would also like to thank my pastor and spiritual covering, Overseer Joseph, for the encouragement, spiritual insight, and professional expertise. You've proven to have the Heart of a Father.

I also want to thank my friend, Janet, for sharing your expert knowledge. I couldn't have completed this project without your fantastic input. You brought it to life.

To all my family, friends, and Pastors' Hubbard's for your support, "thank you." Special shout-out to my cousin Kay, your belief in this project spoke volumes.

FORWARD

Masterfully written, this work possesses the ability to make one experience every emotion God has given to humankind. Isaiah, the prophet, records in the sixty-first chapter, "The Spirit of the Lord God is upon me; because the Lord hath anointed me to preach good tidings unto the meek; he hath sent me to bind up the brokenhearted, to proclaim liberty to the captives, and the opening of the prison to them that are bound;..." This text describes the purpose of this beloved daughter, Bishop Kamia D. White, writings. The taboo surrounding sexuality in the church has driven many who struggle with their sexuality underground. The frustration of this struggle is a snare within their souls, and many are crying to be free. The nature of evil attacks is to derail one from their God-ordained purpose, as a result of the violation, betrayal, self-hate, and a myriad of other offenses. The breach, in turn, affects others who are connected, but the often misdiagnosed root causes mislabeling misunderstanding and confusion. This book provides a template of how God can allow the anointing, which He places within, to come upon and destroy soul ties from without!!! –Church oil, whew!!! (You have to read the book to know what I am talking about...) Riveting! I appeal to every reader to approach this work with an open heart and receive the majestic download of deliverance from Heaven. As one walks through the steps of deliverance, remember Paul's second discourse to the Corinthians in chapter four. He admonishes them on this wise: "We reject all shameful deeds and underhanded methods. We don't try to trick anyone or distort the word of God. We tell the truth before God, and all who are honest know this." (NLT) Truth is not relative, but it is absolute. We must have a willingness to embrace the life-changing truth of God's word and love.

Joseph Edge+, Senior Pastor
Zion Temple Christian Church
Zoe Network of Covenant Churches, General Overseer

__INTRODUCTION__

Introduction

My name is Kamia, and this is my story of a fallen preacher.

The church was a huge part of my life because of my mom's love for God. Early on in life, she instilled Christian values by living the life she taught. There was one thing for sure; God was the center of our home. As a reminder to me, she often shared the story of how the church mothers prayed over me as a baby. The older generation of our church believed in prayer. They were prayer warriors who resolved that God answered them. One night during a prayer service, one of the mothers held me and began to prophesy. Speaking in an unknown tongue, she began to reveal God's plan for my life. His hand was upon my life to do mighty works. It was probably the first time my mother had ever heard a declaration of who I was. My destiny had been sealed before I was ever conceived. It was always very encouraging to listen to what we believed to be the voice of God.

We visited church quite frequently. I often wondered why we attended more than my playmates. Sunday church attendance was all their parents required of them. It never seemed to fail, being next in line to bat, only to be called inside to prepare for church. I promised myself as an adult; I would only attend church on Sundays.

As far as I can remember, I've always loved music. My dad loved to dance, and my mom had a fantastic singing voice. Different genres of music from gospel to soul could be heard ringing throughout the house. At an early age, I sensed that music made people happy. Family gatherings and church events required music to uplift the atmosphere. After these events, I would later reflect upon how the music impacted the atmosphere. These experiences helped to shape my life, and eventually, I choose to become a musician.

My journey as a musician started at the age of fifteen. During my toddler and adolescent years, the church was a huge part of my upbringing. My desire to become a drummer was fueled by watching my mom play the snare. During that time, it was rare to have a keyboardist and a drummer. The snare drum, bass drum, tambourine provided our music. Mom played a mean tap beat on the snare while the other mother held her own with the bass drum. We filled the air with our voices of praise, handclapping, and foot-stomping. Those memories will forever be a part of me.

Music was used by God to help me get to know Him in a personal way. Playing music was my heart's desire. Little did I know that God had called me to work in other areas. Surrendering my life opened the door for instructions. My whole life began to feel as if it was on speed dial. In my quest to understand God and follow His plan, I encountered resistance from the church. I was naïve to the behind the scenes fight to become the most anointed and most liked in ministry. Eventually, I decided to stop following God's instructions. The prophetic gifts upon my life caused chaos.

This decision would prove to be the worst decision of my life. I opted out of obedience for comfort while doing ministry. The Seer gift in my life revealed trouble was coming. The temptation was getting ready to knock at my door with extreme force. My pride dismissed the warning. Several months later, I became involved in a lesbian relationship.

I honestly believe at that time, the enemy began to unravel his plan to keep me from fulfilling my assignment as a Levite. My mother didn't know it then, but I would become one of her most significant prayer assignments. Feelings of inadequacy, guilt, and shame overwhelmed me. I eventually left God and the church. I started a new life away from my past and the church, but God had another plan to redeem me. His Love found me and brought me Home. I am grateful to have a chance to share my losses and victories.

CHAPTER 1

The Beginning

The Beginning

For I am convinced that nothing can ever separate us from His love. Death can't, and life can't. The angels won't, and all the powers of hell itself cannot keep God's love away. Our fears for today, our worries about tomorrow, (39) or where we are – high above the sky, or in the deepest ocean – nothing will ever be able to separate us from the love of God demonstrated by our Lord Jesus Christ when he died for us. Romans 8:38-39 (TLB)

Out of three children conceived, I would be the only survivor. An emergency C-section delivered me. In the sixties, that was huge, and I was born two weeks prematurely. Mom and I both remained in the hospital for over a week after my birth. She thought I was dead because she was not permitted to be near me due to the potential of spreading any illness to me due to my weak immune system. According to my dad, my mom cried for two days because she had no proof that I was alive. Finally, the doctor consented to have me brought to the door of my mom's hospital room so that she could see that her baby was well. I never knew why my mom's other two girls died before birth. I just remembered my mom being depressed and sad that her precious babies did not live. For a mother, there is no deeper sorrow.

I never met my mom's parents; they were deceased long before I was born. With no family near, and my mother still recovering from the C-section, we needed help after my parents brought me home from the hospital. One of my mom's aunts agreed to spend two

13

weeks with us. Smitten by her sister's grandchild, and sensing mom's unspoken cry for continued help, my great aunt never returned to her own home. She would be a constant in my young life, and I grew to love everything about her. She would rise early every morning and quietly move through the house to the kitchen, where she prepared the morning coffee. Her Pentecostal belief system guaranteed us that we would always see her in a beautiful dress, swiftly moving from one task to another. She could effortlessly manage the demands of our home, and spend precious hours tickling me to tears. She quickly became the grandmother I never knew. The countless hours I spent watching ABC soap operas with her cemented our relationship. Our afternoon hours were dedicated to the sacred viewing of All My Children, One Life to Live, and General Hospital. I loved her. She loved me, and I came to love the older generation as a result of the time I spent with her.

Our neighborhood had a lot of kids in it, and that was right up my aunt's alley. They came to our front yard in droves just to play with me and be around my aunt. They loved her, too.

One of the funniest memories I have of growing up happened while I was running through the house. Everyone knew that running inside was not allowed. It was un-lady-like and dangerous. Well, I decided to defy the odds, and sprint from the kitchen, through the dining room, into the dimly lit living room. Halfway through my stunt, I crashed full steam into the china cabinet, knocking myself unconscious. My aunt called my mom, who rushed home from work to take me to the Emergency Room. The only thing that saved me from a much-deserved beat down was the fact that I was already horribly bruised and in considerable pain. I wore the scratches and cuts from that poorly thought out sprint like a suit of armor until my mother showed signs that she had forgotten that I had broken several of her favorite dishes. I'm convinced that every time she thought about retroactively punishing me, my aunt would remind her of how badly I was already injured. Plus, she had a perfect recollection of all of my mom's childhood missteps, and she wasn't beyond using them to get me off the hook. Knowing that you've made a lot of mistakes yourself will calm a temper down really quickly.

Growing up, surrounded by loving and supportive parents. My great aunt added to that feeling of safety and unconditional love. There was never a time I felt abandoned or rejected by them. I was a daddy's girl to the core. As an adult, my mother would tease me about how I would cry to follow him wherever he went. Sometimes he would willingly take me with him for a little while, then bring me back. As a child, a few minutes with the 'right' person can seem like hours. My dad was just that 'right' person for me. He was a short man, but to me, he was a giant. Dressed in the finest suits and smelling of Obsession Cologne, my dad could change the atmosphere of any room by only walking in. He spent his leisure time cheering like crazy for his favorite teams, the Lakers and the Dodgers. Sitting watching the games, cheering when he cheered, booing when he booed. Those were some of the sweetest moments.

When we weren't sharing the joys and heartaches of the battles fought on the basketball court, and the baseball diamond, my dad and I enjoyed each other's company while hunting in the nearby woods or casting our fishing lines in the local river. He was an excellent fisherman, and nothing thrilled me more than spending a Saturday on the river, fishing from his twelve-foot boat. Our goal for the summer was to catch enough fish to send to my grandmother so that she could distribute them to other family members. Under his watchful eye, and to the delight of my entire family, I once caught what seemed like a hundred fish in one afternoon. We ate fish, prepared in every possible way, for days. I skipped through the house, proud to have done so well in front of my dad.

Dad wasn't a professing Christian during my childhood, so his love for dancing to Motown's latest hits was the highlight of our Saturday evenings. I loved to dance with him and watch him show off his version of the newest dance craze as he performed on the linoleum covered kitchen floor. In my early teens, he'd take me to the Elks Club to dance from six o'clock in the evening to eight o'clock at night. By that time, my dance moves were a perfect example of his ability to teach me to dance. The Swing was the favorite dance for both of us, and we twirled and spun around the floor with ease. When our favorite song, "She Used to Be My Girl," sounded across the speakers, the floor was all ours.

He'd bring me home tired and sweaty, laughing at our attempts to out-do the other couples. He wouldn't dance with me on Sundays, though. I guess he didn't want to be disrespectful to the Lord or my mom. Maybe the Lord was already stirring in his heart.

My childhood, up to this point, had been full of what I would call 'routine encounters.' There was a whole lot of laughter and love, and only two or three occasions when I needed and received a whipping from my dad. Being an only child, I spent a great deal of time with my parents and my precious great aunt. My mother's sister would visit us from time to time. We would always repay her visits with our visits to her home. During those visits, we would frequent the nearby restaurants on the weekends. I looked forward to ordering off the menu, tasting foods cooked so differently from the way, my mom cooked them. My mom and her sister had both grown up in a Christian home with strong values. They both experienced times away from God in their adult years. By the time I was born, Mom had dedicated her life back to God. She would suffer some uncertain times, health-wise, and it seemed to me that not a single year went by without her having to spend some time in the hospital.

The year of my twelfth birthday, Mom became very ill. The treatment prescribed by her doctor wasn't available anywhere near our home, so she had to be moved to a hospital several hours away. My dad worked long hours, so it was apparent that he wouldn't be able to take care of me by himself. My great aunt was almost in her eighties by that time, and because her health was beginning to fail, she also needed to be in someone's care. My mom's friend offered to keep me during her hospitalization, but my mom's sister insisted that the responsibility of my care should rest with her. After all, the family takes care of the family. My dad was somewhat apprehensive about allowing me to go with my aunt. During that time, she was dating a man we didn't know anything about, and they were living together. They both had issues, spoken and unspoken. Unspoken problems are the worst.

My daddy's instincts were causing him to worry. Had he made the right decision by allowing my aunt to take care of me while my mom was sick? Dad would always tell me, "Shot, some things are worth going to jail for!" I knew he would do whatever it took to protect his family. He always carried a pocketknife and an ugly stick in his truck. We never traveled out of town in the car without his pistol in the glove compartment. My mom prayed for his safety all the time. So, I know her prayers crushed a lot of terrible things that could have harmed my dad. While she was sick and I was staying with my aunt, Dad must have been doing a whole lot of his own praying.

My great aunt and I stayed with my aunt during the weekdays. Our routine on the weekends included staying with my dad and visiting Mom in Lakeland, Florida. That was a tough time for me. I'd never seen Mom in that condition. She was unable to walk without the assistance of a walker or crutches. The local doctors sent her to a specialized clinic to receive additional help.

I was scared, not knowing if my mom would ever be able to walk again without some assistance. The one thing I must say about "Mother White" was that she was a woman of strong unfailing faith. My mom was going to believe God until the breakthrough manifested.

During the week, my aunt and her boyfriend drank alcohol heavily. He would also smoke marijuana. I could always tell when he was planning to get high. Before smoking, he would change out of his regular clothes and put on an all-black outfit with dark shades. I never understood why he did that, but it always made me feel uncomfortable. My aunt was intoxicated, sleep, and passed out most nights. Unaware of his behavior.

One night the three of us were sitting at the kitchen table playing cards. My aunt was heavily intoxicated and could barely focus on the game. While she was concentrating on her drink, her boyfriend stretched out his leg and touched my inner thigh with his foot. He sat there across the table, staring at me, waiting for me to respond. I couldn't alert my aunt because she was already intoxicated. Later that night, I was watching television while my aunt was sleeping. I began to feel uncomfortable being alone with her boyfriend. He approached me and asked if I had ever been fu****. I didn't understand what he was asking me; I had never heard the word used that way before. He then began to explain the process. He promised that he wouldn't hurt me, but I said no. I was terrified, and I felt trapped. There was no one there to protect or comfort me.

My aunt was passed out drunk, and my great aunt was asleep in her bedroom with the door closed. I decided to sit in my aunt's bedroom and watch television until she woke up. I was hoping that it wouldn't take a long time. A few minutes later, after I sat down in front of the television, her boyfriend came into the room and laid down on the bed beside my still unconscious aunt. The next few minutes have remained in my memory no matter how hard I've tried to forget them. To my horror, he began to masturbate and ejaculate, trying to entice me to have sex with him. I didn't know what to think or do at that point. I got up and ran to my great aunt's bedroom. The next day, I was visibly shaken by the experience. My aunt, noticing the change in my behavior, began asking me if there was anything wrong. I remember trying to figure out if I should tell her what happened while she was drunk. Her boyfriend said to me that nobody would believe me. He threatened to tell everybody that I wanted to lose my virginity. After a couple of days, I decided to break my silence and tell her everything that had happened. She didn't believe me. She denied that I had experienced everything I told her. She said it was just a misunderstanding and that her boyfriend would never do anything like that. Crushed, I felt as though I'd made a big mistake by sharing what happened that night.

The next day, my dad picked up my great aunt and me for dinner. I tried really hard to be my usual happy smiling self on the way to dinner. All that day, I had been practicing how I would smile and laugh so he wouldn't know there was something wrong. I was working on acting as if everything was okay because I knew my dad wouldn't mind going to jail over what I was hiding. I could picture him sitting behind bars, crying because he would never see my mother or me again as a free man. I would do whatever I could to keep that from happening. But, he wasn't fooled at all by my act. As soon as we pulled away from my aunt's house, he began drilling me with questions about what was wrong, and about what had happened to me. I made him promise that he wouldn't harm anyone or do anything that would cause him to go to jail. He promised that he would remain calm. Knowing that my great aunt, who was frail and up in years, wouldn't be able to take the horror of my secret, I promised my dad I would tell him everything.

Now that we were alone, I began to explain what I'd experienced the night before. Crying, I told him that I was scared and that I didn't want to go back to my aunt's house. The expression on my dad's face was unforgettable. He apologized to me, explaining that he had made a promise that he couldn't keep. I cried uncontrollably, begging him not to shoot my aunt's boyfriend. He finally gathered himself, released his grip on the steering wheel, and with tears in his eyes, told me that I wouldn't be going back to my aunt's house. We didn't get dinner that night. My dad spent the rest of the evening packing my, and my great aunt's things in his car. He worked feverishly without saying a word. Just like he said, I never went back to that house. Later that night, my dad started learning how to style my hair. The hairstyle was rough, but after the chaos of my aunt's house, it was okay with me. Being home, in a safe environment was all that mattered at the time.

My life was deeply affected by the trauma of that experience. I began to hate my aunt and her boyfriend. I was too young to separate them from their soul tie, which was in a destructive state. There was a sense of betrayal, and it affected how I made decisions later in life.

My mom arrived home after being hospitalized for three weeks. Although I was ecstatic about her being home, I battled replays of those past events. Dad and I decided we wouldn't share the situation with my mom. We didn't want her to feel guilty about being sick and having to place me with my aunt. Mom's recovery was our most pressing concern. It was years later that I discovered that Mom was a Seer. I genuinely believe God revealed to her that there was a level of anger and disappointment between me, Dad, and her sister. Finally, after Mom showed significant signs of improvement, I spilled the beans. She cried, and I felt horrible as if it were all my fault. She held me and reassured me that I had done nothing to deserve what happened. In her infinite wisdom, she stated that my aunt was afraid, too, and that she loved me. It sounded good, but I struggled to believe it. All I knew was that, afraid or not, she had chosen him.

After revealing the situation to Mom, Dad restricted us from visiting my aunt at her house. Of course, that didn't last very long; Mom started visiting her alone. I never went back to my aunt's house. The fear of having to face her boyfriend overrode any family obligation I might have felt. Eventually, the relationship between my aunt and her boyfriend collapsed. The Lord restored my aunt, and she would later become a minister of the Gospel. Mother White, my mom, was an anointed prayer warrior. I believe she bombarded heaven for a total recovery for my aunt. She was released from a life of addiction and domestic violence.

Mom was very protective when it came to sleepovers away from home. Between the ages of five and fourteen, I wasn't allowed to stay over a friend's house. Slumber parties were only permitted when multiple girls were coming, and the hosting girl's mother had to be there to supervise the entire time. During the day was when I spent time playing with other kids. Our street was full of kids of all ages, from insecure toddlers to confident teens. I guess you could say our street was famous. It was definitely the place to be. Our favorite games to play were Fumble, Playhouse, Doctor, and Church. We played them all the time. The younger set of kids played house and cooked mud pies to bake in the summer heat. While their little pies dried on the sidewalk, they played Dress Up. The older kids took it a step further. I must admit that it was during those early years that I began to understand that there was more to playing house than cooking mud pies and dressing up. Some of the things we began to experience started to wake up desires before most of us had reached puberty.

If my mom had known about the activities going on in the church playhouse and the block playhouse, I would have been playing by myself.

In my pre-teen years, sexuality wasn't a topic of discussion between my mom and me. As I began to show signs of maturing, my mom sat me down and told me that I would soon have a menstrual cycle. She explained that this would allow me to become a mother after I married. She made sure I understood that marriage was a non-negotiable requirement for motherhood.

I have fond memories of those years of physical change. In my adolescent years, my family consisted pretty much of all boys. Funny stories are always remembered. Whenever my uncle kept us, we played football in the front yard. Since I was the only girl, I had to play whatever the boys wanted to play. I was completely unaware of the stages of puberty, so it never occurred to me to be careful with my body. My cousins and I had been playing tackle football together for a couple of years. I was proud of the fact that I was a girl, and I was good enough to play with them. It was tough. I remember playing with them one summer day. The game was getting good until I got tackled hard, and I fell on my stomach. I hit the ground hard, and a sharp pain raged through my chest. My uncle picked me up and carried me into the house. That was the day I realized that my body was changing. So, we started playing tag football. At the age of eleven, I was maturing and growing breasts. Everything changed.

During my young teenage years, homosexuality was a word that was not common. The term 'homosexuality' was never really used among my family, church circle, or friends. When I look back on the initial years of my puberty, having crushes on boys was in full force. I had boyfriends throughout my elementary and middle school years.

During orientation for middle school, I found out that I could learn how to play drums in the school band. I was extremely excited by this information. Watching my mom play the snare at church had a significant influence on my choice of instrument. I was grateful to my parents for encouraging me to learn what wasn't usually accessible to girls. Mom wasn't the kind of person who could be swayed by doubters. When her family was against her marrying my dad, she followed her heart. So, the opposition didn't matter if she believed it was the right decision. One of my mom's aunts thought I should play the flute or the clarinet, and she had no problem voicing her opinion about my desire to play the drums. Mom's side of the family could be bossy and critical at the same time. Again, Mom would not change her mind.

I will always remember my middle school band teacher. He was friendly, talented, and very influential. As a girl, it was difficult coming into an environment where only the boys played drums. Sometimes I would be afraid to play in front of them. They were confident in their abilities, and their confidence sometimes shook mine. But my teacher always told me I could do it. He never doubted me

Beginning Band was where everyone started. I believed that God's hand was upon me, and I quickly excelled in the advanced group by my seventh-grade year. My parents were so proud of me and of the choice they'd made when they allowed me to follow my dream. They never missed a band concert. They were there to witness my steady improvement as a percussionist, becoming second chair snare in Advanced Band. Mom attended every parade, impressed by her baby. Whew! Playing drums in a five-mile show is a lot of work. I was exhausted after every event; it always took me a couple of hours to recover. Everything was going well, except my peers said girls didn't play five-piece drum sets. Unfortunately, I became fearful and never learned how to play a full drum set.

I signed up for the band at the high school in my ninth grade year. Boy, was I in for a total shock! The band instructor was not a fan of up to date music. His choice of music was mostly classical. The Marching Band was the best thing going. It was great traveling with the football team and playing the Toms. Eventually, I decided that I no longer wanted to be part of the high school band.

At the age of fifteen, I started singing with our church youth choir. It was a lot of fun having a Sunday that was designated for the youth to perform. We traveled quite a bit. My Father in the Lord was our Assistant Pastor and organist at the time. His skills as a musician were terrific for a man in his forties. He played drums, keys, bass, sax, and guitar, to name a few.

Those were enjoyable experiences for me, and my love for playing the drums ignited once again.

I was traveling from church to church, allowing me to see drummers of all ages play. They were great drummers, even the ones who were younger than I was. My heart desired to play a five-piece set for God, and that desire increased daily. It was all I could think about, wishing I had a drum set of my own to practice on and play. I finally gathered enough courage to ask my mom to purchase a set of drums for me. That was a bold step for me since I never learned how to play acoustic drums while I was in middle school. I prayed that mom wouldn't base her decision on the fact that I had already wasted one opportunity to make my dream come true.

To my surprise, my parents purchased an old used Ludwig five-piece drum set for a hundred and fifty dollars. Man, talking about being excited! Somehow I mustered up enough faith to believe if I practiced God would anoint my ability. The Spring of 1982 was the beginning of long hours of practice.

Mom was so considerate of others that my practice time was restricted and starting after 2 P.M. and ending at 8 P.M. The practice routine consisted of duplicating the drummers on gospel records. Learning how to keep the pace of a song was challenging for me, especially if the tempo was fast.

Mom was a trooper through this phase. Some evenings she would join me by playing her tambourine and singing along to help me keep the tempo. There were many days it appeared as if I would never get it. I was so serious about learning how to play; all my extra time was spent rehearsing. My schedule consisted of no less than two hours every day, including weekends. I was determined to do what my peers said I couldn't do. I had something to prove to them and myself.

I was so excited about attending church every Sunday. I sat in the congregation, hearing the music, and secretly dreaming I was playing along. No one knew I was learning to play at home. Suddenly, my mom couldn't keep the secret anymore. Proudly, she told our Assistant Pastor, who played the organ every Sunday, and the Pastor, that I knew how to play. Oh, my God! Why did she say that! The Assistant Pastor then proceeded to ask me to start playing at our church. He was my Father in the Lord, and I had always dreamed of playing along with him as he played the organ every Sunday. I couldn't and didn't want to refuse him. I had practiced faithfully to recorded songs, but I had never had the chance to play with a live band. The church musicians were excellent, just as good as some of the bands I heard on the records I listened to and practiced with at home. I certainly didn't want to mess up in front of them. The thought of that made me nervous, but the idea of playing with them was beyond exciting. I was anxious and restless the whole week leading up to that next Sunday. I practiced extra hours every day that week. I wanted more than anything to be ready.

Finally, the moment I had anticipated! The day of my debut as the church drummer had arrived. It was time for the first song. I moved from my regular seat, sat on the drummer's stool, wiped my sweaty palms on my skirt, and then picked up the drumsticks. I could hear people mumbling and whispering behind their paper fans, wondering why I was on the drummer's stool. When I listened to the organ playing, that gave me the signal to join in the playing of the mid-tempo song. I froze. Everything I had learned over the past six months forgotten in an instant. Fear grabbed my mind, paralyzed my hands, and made it so that I couldn't produce anything I had practiced and learned. My beloved Father in the Lord saved the day. He got up from his seat at the organ in the middle of the song, calmly walked over to me, took the drumsticks from my frozen hands, and began playing the song for me. That simple act gave me courage. After about a minute of playing, he gave the sticks back to me and said, "Now, you can do it." He was right. I played, just like I had practiced. I will never forget what he did for me at that moment. It was as if he spoke to the anxiety I felt, and I miraculously gained the courage to play. As time went on, I became more confident as I played for our church.

My next challenge was playing in front of experienced drummers. Watching these guys play, with their five to ten years of experience, was overwhelming for me. My skillset was nowhere near the ballpark of theirs. Also, I still battled with the belief that my being a female somehow limited my ability to play. Starting on the drums at the age of sixteen was very rare. The realization that, by that age, most of the young musicians had already moved on to another instrument.

A lot of the church musicians had started as young drummers. I had so many emotional hurdles to jump.

The Lord had a plan for my life, and fear was going to be defeated. A local revival invited us to sing. Three different excellent drummers played, especially the eighteen-year-old. My heart just pounded as it got closer to my turn to play. As you probably already guessed, I froze again, couldn't play! My mom, determined to push me, punished me after that service for not playing. I couldn't have any phone privileges for an entire week. Can you imagine being a sixteen-year-old girl with no phone privileges? I thought that was cruel and unusual punishment. Wasn't the shame and embarrassment punishment enough? Mom must have known it wasn't.

Instantly, I was healed! Never again did I refuse to play because of fear. I probably sound like a broken record, but Mother White was a leader and a pusher. Her faith exercised when you didn't have any. There aren't enough words to describe my mom's influence. The best thing I can do is give to others what she gave me courage.

I can't forget to mention how God supernaturally increased my ability. Mom and I spent a great deal of time praying and fasting, and God was faithful. He even began to give me strategies to help improve my stamina while playing the drums. Playing for a Pentecostal church required strength, and some of the rhythms were very fast. One of the techniques was to play along with fast tempo music for an hour. The Lord gave me fantastic tools to combat fatigue. Also, a three-pound weight helped develop strength in my muscles for speed.

CHAPTER 2

The Call

The Call

The Gospel of Jesus Christ was a priority in the church. Although I hadn't surrendered my life, I knew the importance of it. My desire to become a drummer also helped draw me closer to salvation. Mom had always encouraged me to give my life to the Lord. She lived in such a way before me that I wanted the joy and peace she had. Also, I believe that God marks you if He wants to use you, and sometimes that causes you to stand out, even when you aren't trying to be noticed or recognized. That marking, or setting apart, makes you peculiar. I had a few friends from church that I hung out with at school. We were known as the "Holy Rollers" because it was commonly known that our church members spoke in tongues, dressed modestly, and we didn't hang out with just anybody. That didn't stop some people from trying to get us to be who they wanted us to be.

During my tenth-grade year in high school, my boyfriend was a musician who lived out of town. We liked each other a lot, but we didn't get to see each other often. One day I was approached by a ninth-grader who wanted my phone number for a friend. I asked why their friend was interested in reaching me. He replied I had an admirer. I tried to ignore that request the first day, but he continued to ask me for my number to give to this secret admirer. I believe my inquisitiveness got the best of me. All-day, I carefully watched the boys in my classes, in the hallway, and the cafeteria. I was hoping to catch my admirer watching me. None of them seemed to pay me any extra attention, so I finally slid a folded up piece of paper across the cafeteria table to my secret admirer's messenger.

The next day I received a call from an older female, stating that she was interested in dating me. Now, this was the shock of my life! Immediately, I defended my belief system and responded with, "I am not interested!" It seemed as if the more I resisted, the more she tried to sway my stance. She presented all kinds of arguments against my answer, questioning me about how I was so sure I wouldn't like it. The whole idea of it was just outrageous to me. I asked her what made her think I would be interested in dating a woman. Her answer startled me. I had attended a wake service with my aunt a few months before all this happened. I didn't really know the deceased. I just went along for moral support. I had no idea he was gay, or that my secret admirer was there that day. When she saw me at the funeral, she associated me with the lesbian lifestyle. Even after I told her I wasn't interested, she continued to pursue me for a few years. She began to stalk me, showing up at my job, and continually asking if I would give her a chance to make me happy. I was stunned and concerned that I might have acted in a way that made her think I was a lesbian.

The next incident was very subtle, but now that I look back, I was slowly being groomed to live my life as a lesbian. Mother White was always looking out for the youth. She was a protector, as well as a Seer. God would show her danger and quite a few other things.

She was aware of situations never mentioned. I didn't understand that the call of a Seer was also upon life. Would God also show me dangers?

Among my peers, there were a few of us who hung out together more often. Some of us attended the same school, so we'd eat lunch together every day. Our daily routine included speaking to each other on the phone, writing notes to each other, and eating lunch together. Everyone pretty much-shared lunch with the same crew every day. There wasn't anything awkward about our friendship. Most of our girlfriends followed the same daily pattern of communication. We were no different.

One day, I decided to eat with some other friends. We had forty minutes for lunch, and I spent about twenty minutes with them. After sharing a few laughs, I decided I was going to look for my other friend and finish the rest of my lunchtime with her. When I found her, she was so angry with me that she knocked my food out of my hands. We exchanged angry words and stopped speaking to each other for a few days. About a week later, Mom overheard me in a heated phone conversation with her. I was just trying to move forward from the lunch incident. Shocked to listen to me arguing with my best friend, Mom shouted, "You two sound as if you are dating!" I had no response to her comment. Our lunchtime disagreement redefined our friendship. Although there wasn't any discussion of us being anything more than friends, the whole situation made us feel uncomfortable. Eventually, my friend and I grew apart, but we remained loosely connected as we got older. I went on with my life and still never considered myself a lesbian.

Things began to speed up in my teenage life. I was asked to share a testimony during a special event for our Assistant Pastor. That was huge for me because I struggled with being shy. Getting up to speak in front of a room full of people made me sick to my stomach. Overcoming the fear of playing the drums wasn't the same type of fear that came along with speaking publicly. Talking to my mom, getting suggestions on what to say and how to present it, really helped me. I had seen her speak in front of a crowd many times, and I learned a lot from those public speaking events. Talking to people seemed to come naturally to her. She always displayed confidence and gave relevant information. I wanted to be able to do that. I practiced in front of the mirror, hoping to master that same easy conversational approach my mom used.

The time for my Assistant Pastor's appreciation event was quickly approaching. Before I knew it, it was time for me to, once again, show what I had been practicing. There are a few moments in my life that stand out. That night goes down in my memory bank. The program had at least ten participants, and I was about the fifth one scheduled to make a presentation. Everyone was so grateful for the opportunity to be a blessing to our leader. He was more of a community Pastor, and he generously shared his gift with others. We wanted him to know how big of an impact his ministry was having on our lives and our Christian walk. Like everybody else, I really wanted to do a good job.

The closer it got to my turn to speak, the more nervous I became. I could feel my throat tightening and my palms sweating. I gave the written copy of my speech one last look. The funny thing about my testimony was that I gave it a title! Who does that for a declaration? The title was, "Don't Get Saved for the Wrong Reason."

When it was time for me to present what I had written, I shared that I wanted to be like the young adults who had already given their lives to the Lord. Peer pressure was real, even back then. If they weren't careful, they could easily be led down the wrong path. Giving my life to the Lord allowed their parents to trust me more. Knowing that I was saved put their parents at ease with me, and I was allowed into their close-knit circle of friends. I stated that eventually, it became a struggle to live as a Christian because my reason for choosing Christianity wasn't sincere. Through the voice of a friend who formed a Christian Contemporary Singing Group, it became clear to me that Salvation was more important than anything. It would also be a vital part of the ministry of being a percussionist. It was then that I began to pray and read my bible to gain a personal relationship with Jesus. Like an overturned cup, everything spilled out of me in front of the crowd.

Everyone was very receptive to what I had to say, and they encouraged me to continue to stay with God. The appreciation program ended with dinner. I was so happy the event was over, and I just wanted some refreshments. Well, God had another plan for me that evening. Walking toward the kitchen, one of the youth mentors stopped me. With minimal small talk, she said: "You are called to preach the Gospel."

The look on my face must have been priceless. In my mind, I was thinking, 'she's got to be kidding, right!' I was so shocked; all I could say was, "No, ma'am, I was only sharing my testimony." She proceeded to tell me that she had the gift to See and that the call of God was upon my life. It felt as if the whole world had stopped! She also said that the anointing of God was upon my testimony in a significant way. After that unexpected conversation, I was in a state of shock. My physical appetite left the building while I tried to digest the words spoken to me. There wasn't room for both.

My mind couldn't comprehend the Word of the Lord. Why would God call a girl who struggled to speak publicly, not to mention the fact that I was only sixteen! I never shared this information with anyone, fearing I would be made to follow through on what had been spoken over my life. My relationship with the Lord continued to grow. I became president of our teen Christian singing group and chaplain for our high school's basketball team. While my attention focused on all my new responsibilities, God was grooming me for His Will. Of course, I questioned the appointments as well. My shyness always made me feel as though I was inadequate. God began to surround me with spiritual leaders, along with Mom.

One day, while praying on my knees, I believed I heard the voice of God. I was still a babe in Christ, so learning to recognize the voice of God was ongoing. A clear voice said, "I've called you into the ministry." Another moment where my faith was asking a question. Could what the youth mentor told me a few months ago have been right? Well, I decided that when I got a chance, I'd visit with a body of believers who were known to have operated in the prophetic. They were trusted voices. A couple of months passed, then finally, I visited their church. The service was terrific, and it was almost over when they called my name. The Prophetess called me to the altar for prayer. She said the Lord had called me into the ministry. She touched my hands and said they were anointed. Moments like this were used by God to define my life.

I was relieved that the youth mentor and I had really heard from God. While thankful, I was also scared to death. Preaching was never a thought or desire of mine. Playing drums was all I wanted to do for the Lord. Figuring out the call to preach was very challenging for me. I kept quiet about it for months. There was no guide available for young preachers to follow. I knew the proper protocol required that I speak with my Senior Leader for acknowledgment and further instructions. New ministry candidates didn't have mentorship classes available to them. For me, my mom was the closest designated mentor. Her prayer life and her faith in God was a lesson all by itself. I had seen her cry out to the Lord many times, believing Him for the impossible. God had never failed her, and I thought He would be just as faithful to me.

Finally, I felt it was time to meet with my Senior Leader about the call of God on my life. I didn't know what to expect, but I knew this was the right step. As I shared my experiences of what I believed to be God's voice calling me, I was shaking in my boots. The response I received from my senior leader was short and straight to the point. He listened to what I had to say, then quietly, he responded by saying, "Okay, Sister White. If it is God, it will last. And, if not, it won't".

I waited for more instructions from him, but there wasn't any. I heard my shaky voice say, "Yes, Sir." He scheduled me to present my trial sermon the next month on Youth Sunday. With that, our conversation was officially over.

Life was moving so fast for me. Every time I thought about everything that was in front of me, I wanted to scream, 'Whoa God! Now I am studying the scripture to encourage others, and I'm drumming, questioning my salvation, and teaching the Word of the Lord. Why me, Lord? I guess I'll get that answer when I get to Heaven'. The Christian Bookstore became my friend. While studying and praying about my upcoming trial sermon, I was impressed by the Lord to write my outline as if I were writing an essay. My format included an introduction, a thesis statement, three points, and a conclusion that included an argument to bring the topic to a close. That format made sense to me, so I was hoping and praying that it would make sense to everyone who was listening to me.

Even though Mother White was ecstatic about the fact that I had been assigned the upcoming Youth Sunday to present my trial sermon, I started thinking that maybe I hadn't heard from God. Fear began to try to overtake my mind, and anxiety kept telling me that I wouldn't be able to teach with clarity or power. I had to press beyond thoughts of failure. Praying was the ultimate weapon that gave me the strength to stand before the people. Our senior leader introduced me as an upcoming speaker and stated that he had approved the call of God upon my life. I became known as the youth speaker at our church. My journey of learning how to share the word of God with others was an ongoing process. I am grateful for the patience shown to me while I was trying to figure out how to become the person I thought I was supposed to be.

The process wasn't easy or short. I did a whole lot of praying to God, asking for instruction and guidance. Learning to recognize the Lord's voice was a primary concern for me. With limited experience in discerning God's voice, I placed that as my priority. Growing up in the church had allowed me to hear and watch a lot of preachers as they ministered to the needs of their waiting congregations. I had noticed that one of the most popular things rehearsed by preachers was the ability to be led by God through His instruction. I wanted to hear God and be able to speak to Him more than anything. Having a relationship with Him was precious to me.

Being confident to speak His Word was undergirded and supported by my relationship with Him outside of the pulpit. The more time I spent in the presence of God, the easier it became for me to recognize His voice and understand scriptures.

Preaching to a familiar audience was a huge advantage to me. Standing before people who had watched me grow, both physically and spiritually, provided me with a cushion. One Sunday, I was teaching about Peter, the fisherman called by Jesus. During my delivery, the saints nodded and gave their "Amen," as a sign that they agreed with what I said. Later that evening, the Holy Spirit prompted me to go back and read the text concerning Peter's first encounter with Christ. To my horror, I realized that I had taught that Simon Peter was two separate people. It was after I went back to review the scripture that I realized that Simon Peter is the name of one person. I am sure the congregation heard the mistake I made, but because I was young and unskilled, they never crucified me or approached me about it later. I was extremely embarrassed after finding out my blooper. It was a humbling experience that taught me that even intentionally gifted people are not beyond mistakes. When I told my mom, she laughed and said, "That's alright baby, you're doing a good job." This experience also falls under that category of 'Unforgettable Moments.'

CHAPTER 3

Balancing Act

Balancing Act

   While growing in my relationship with the Lord, my drumming skills were improving. I even felt confident enough in my skillset to teach three of my friends from the church how to play. To have four female drummers, all under the age of eighteen, was unheard of in that day. We were engulfed in music because we were encouraged to expand our gifts. We traveled from Miami to all parts of North Carolina to sing and play music. The Lord also blessed us with an opportunity to share our talents on a televised gospel program. They featured our youth choir and the Contemporary Christian Ensemble. What an exciting time that was for us! My mom played a very significant role in the lives of the youth of our church, and the newly established Contemporary group. She, along with my Father in the Lord, served as the spiritual advisors for both groups. They made a fantastic team as they imparted our lives with truth and the unconditional love of God. They were the catalyst for a lot of things that have taken place in our lives over the years. Many of us became professional musicians, Pastors, Bishops, and leaders in the secular industry.

   While being a junior, preparing for my senior year in high school, I was happy with what God was doing in my life. Having a boyfriend who understood my commitment to God was absolutely necessary. The trend among singers and musicians seemed to be to date someone who was also musically inclined. That meant that we usually ended up dating someone with very similar interests and opinions about the things that really mattered. Based on my personal history, this was true. My previous boyfriend had been a bassist and organist. After we broke up, I started dating a drummer. He was a couple of years younger than I was, but that didn't bother me. He was a nice guy, and I learned a lot from him. Drumming was his passion, and it showed in the way he played. One night we decided to attend a revival service at his church. Secretly, I had asked the Lord for a deeper measure of His Spirit. We were sitting on the fourth row from the back of the church. Well, the Lord showed up that night like a whirlwind! All I can remember is standing up, clapping my hands; after that, everything else was a blur. I remember thinking, 'what in the world just happened; how did I get to the front of the church?' It seems as if all eyes were on me as I began getting up from the floor. My mom was there and smiled over me, knowing what had happened to me. That night, my life shifted once again, spiritually.

My church friends started teasing me big time! I became known as the drummer, who would throw sticks and shout. Shouting music with no drums wasn't enough to stop my praise. Thank God, there was always another drummer in the house, and because everybody knew I was prone to dancing whenever the Spirit hit me, there was usually no break in the rhythm of the music whenever I threw down my sticks. The next drummer would seamlessly ease onto the stool and quickly pick up the beat of the music while I danced before the Lord.

God uniquely used my dance. Many times, it seemed as if people were quenching the Spirit. I would often be the first dancer, and then suddenly, the fire of God would begin to touch others. The next thing you know, there were dancers and worshippers all over the place. A prophet once told me that God had anointed my dance to break strongholds. That went way over my head! I had heard the word 'stronghold' used before, but I didn't understand what they were. All I knew was that when the Spirit hit me, nothing could hold me in my seat. God had been so good to me.

Being a high school Senior, taking part in two musical groups, playing drums for my church, and holding down a job was a lot of responsibility. To add to a busy life, I also started dating a new guy. You guessed it; he was also a musician. When I look back, I don't know how I did it all. With all that going on, there was still a pang of hunger in me for more of God's Spirit. One of our Elders began teaching on the gift of tongues. He was so convincing when he spoke about the availability of this gift that we all believed that speaking in other tongues was for any believer who truly wanted it. It wasn't just for special people in the body of Christ. According to the Elder, we could receive it by faith. I never forgot what I heard. I started thanking God every day for blessing me with my prayer language. I exercised my faith and honestly believed that one day I would receive my tongues.

Shortly after hearing the Elder's teaching, a friend invited me to attend their Easter service. The Holy Spirit charged the service from the beginning to the end. It's a day I will never forget, April 22, 1984. The Pastor preached a dynamic sermon on the power of the resurrection. As he taught, the people began to dance under the influence of God. I remember dancing, but not much else about the events after the sermon. I began to raise my hands, and the tears flowed uncontrollably down my cheeks. As I continued to worship, I began to feel as if my stomach was quivering. I'd never experienced that kind of feeling before. Suddenly, the quivering seemed to travel up and out of my mouth. The gift of tongues flowed freely off my lips. The power of the Holy Spirit consumed me so until I cried and spoke in tongues all the way home. I knew I would never be the same. God had blessed me with my heart's desire. Having my prayer language would increase my understanding and my ability to do ministry. We were all taught to remain humble while doing ministry. We understood that it was only through God that we receive the strength and the knowledge required to do the work of the ministry.

After receiving my prayer language, the spirit realm began to manifest in a way I'd never experienced before. Hearing God's heart, or the instructions He was giving me, became more evident. At first, I was afraid because I had not been to a place where I felt so strongly about our communication. The time that I was spending in prayer, praying in tongues, was adding to my life. My walk with Christ shifted to a place I couldn't comprehend with my natural mind. It was definitely new ground for me, and I was so excited about what I had begun to experience.

One of the first things I noticed after receiving my prayer language was that I began to dream more frequently, and I remembered the entire dream. Before my experience, there was only one dream I could remember. The visions increased tremendously, and I was able to remember them all, and they followed a pattern. They were mostly about sickness, snakes, water, death, and demons. There would always be a strong sense of needing to pray about what I'd seen. Intercession birthed consistent prayer.

With little knowledge, I began to write down the dreams I wanted to keep for prayer, as God would lead me. While growing in prayer, God began to instruct me to share the visuals and pray for people. I had no idea the Prophetic Mantle upon my life was being groomed. God's voice became even more resolved about how to pray and minister to others.

Dreams and visions were also working in my personal life. During my senior year, I began to date a friend from our Contemporary band in the summer of 1984. I was a virgin, and I was committed to living a lifestyle of Holiness. We held hands, kissed, and embraced, but never anything more. In November of that same year, I had a vision of my boyfriend kissing another woman while he was overseas. I prayed about it, but I wasn't sure how to handle the situation. Little did I know, but God had another plan in store.

While visiting his family and me during the Christmas Holidays, we attended church together. That night my Pastor was conducting a revival at another church. The power of God was moving while Pastor preached. Out of nowhere, he said, "You could be in Germany, and God still sees what you are doing." After the service, my boyfriend wanted to talk. He told me that the message was for him. He confessed there was another woman in his life. He began to apologize and explain that he didn't want to be alone. A marriage proposal followed the apology.

Now I had to figure out how I was going to tell my parents about my boyfriend's intention to marry me. He decided to do it the traditional way and ask my father if he could marry me. I wasn't sure how that would turn out because I was a daddy's girl to the core. He was very protective of me, and he wasn't going to take any junk. When my boyfriend finally wrestled up the courage to ask my dad if he could marry me, my dad made him promise two things. The first thing was that my college education was to be paid. The second thing was if he ever got tired of me, he was to contact my father for a flight home for me. My boyfriend agreed to those two conditions. So, in January 1985, I officially became engaged. Everything seemed to be going well. I loved him and trusted that he would abstain from sex until we were married. I waited for him to come back to the states in January of 1986.

We finalized wedding plans and had everything but my dress. We planned to shop together in March. In a night vision, I saw him with another woman just before he arrived home in the states. This time, my heart was broken, and I felt like he couldn't be trusted. My emotions overcame me, and I couldn't hide that there was something wrong. Eventually, after being questioned, I told my fiancé what God showed me. Our engagement ended; that was the last straw. We tried to continue the relationship, but I couldn't get past the hurt. How would I ever be able to trust him?

It had been a few months since the engagement ended when I felt an unction from the Lord to seek out further counsel and instruction on how to use the gifts I'd received. Searching Christian bookstores, I found "Understanding the Anointing," by the late Kenneth E. Hagin. I was convinced that God had led me to this much-needed source of information. I was operating in my spiritual gifts to the best of my knowledge. Honestly, there were times when I felt a little weird because no one else seemed to be experiencing these knowing moments. Reading the book gave me peace in the knowledge that these encounters were real, and God was leading me.

Growing in grace to bless others just felt as if it was what I was called to do. Watching people receive help and freedom gave me so much joy. Eventually, I began to have prayer meetings with my friends from church. We were all experiencing God on levels that expanded our worship. God also used the musical gifts and talents He had given us to usher in His presence among the people. My Spiritual Father sent letters to the local churches about a choir he was starting. Mother White also played a very intricate part in helping to maintain the choir as well. Being officers and directors of the choir gave us opportunities to share our gifts with young adults. The community choir began to travel all over the state and even up north.

Although we were a choir made up of many different churches, we operated like one church. You couldn't tell if those participating were Baptist, Methodist, Catholic, or Pentecostal. The presence of God would manifest powerfully among us, even during our rehearsals. The choir wasn't traditional by any means. As far as I knew, it wasn't an everyday thing to see a choir with a young girl as the drummer, a grey head keyboardist, a Caucasian man on guitar, and two teenagers playing brass. If you're thinking we looked funny; you're absolutely correct. After arriving at most churches, we were laughed at and sometimes picked on over the microphone by the person who introduced us. We were never bothered by what the people thought of us or said about us. We knew something they didn't know; the Lord was with us.

I'll never forget the time we ministered at a Choir Anniversary. We were the special guest. We called ourselves the Love Fellowship Community Choir. There were other groups on the program to perform, but we ministered six songs. We could hear the snickers coming from the audience as we approached the choir stand. Our first selection was a song performed acapella. One of our dear brothers traveled with us and directed this

51

song. The audience anticipated a flop, but our God did not disappoint us. His presence overwhelmed the church as we bellowed out the first words of the song. The pulpit guest, including the Pastor, left the pulpit area because our voices sounded like trumpets behind their heads. The audience screamed and clapped to show their amazement and approval of this unknown choir from a small town. Listen, that's just one story of how people underestimated us due to the age range of the singers and the looks of the band. Whenever and wherever we ministered, God always showed up and blessed the people tremendously.

CHAPTER 4

The Impact of the Choir

The Impact of the Choir

My Father in the Lord never required that participants in the choir be Christians. Many of the saints in our circle disapproved of that idea. They often stated their opinions about how the choir should have held a higher standard for membership. My Father in the Lord shared the gospel with the choir to influence them to choose Jesus as their savior. It was an excellent evangelizing tool. In 1986 I was voted president of the choir. The Lord used this time to develop me in the revelation gifts. Sometimes I'd give a word of encouragement to our choir, often laying hands on them, praying for all their needs. God was revealing many different situations involving choir members. His revealing of dangers, demons, and traps involving our choir members would become part of my life.

One night, during a night vision, I saw a choir member's car parked in an unknown parking lot. I also saw a snake underneath her vehicle. God instructed me to pray for her at the next choir rehearsal. I was to pray that no danger would come to her. The following Monday, I prayed to God for protection from the hand of the enemy. Two weeks later, she testified that a co-worker had forged her name on some relevant paperwork. The plan was to set her up for termination. The documents were examined, and the signature was determined to be a forgery. Praise and honor to God broke out during rehearsal. Although we were far from perfect, the hand of God was saving and filling people with the Holy Spirit. There were times when we couldn't rehearse because God's glory would overpower us. People began to ask if they could come and sit in on our rehearsals because of the presence of God we were encountering.

As God was using the choir as my training ground, I began to feel better about what I was being asked to do. Seeing the outcomes, based on my obedience, gave me great joy and even greater reverence for our God.

The Love Fellowship Choir was made up of families. Our love for each other grew, and we supported each other, even outside the choir. It felt more like one big happy family, who traveled together from time to time.

I had just turned twenty years old, and my life seemed to be taking another turn. Now I'm being asked to preach at places other than my home church. The new territory was a different ballgame for me. While I was getting familiar with my own church family, I was also going to new churches. When I sat down and gave it some thought about what I was doing, fear attacked my mind, telling me that I wasn't ready to preach to others. After prayer and careful consideration, I stepped out on faith and accepted invitations from other churches, as my Pastor released me to go. Many of those assignments were to the youth on their particular Sunday. I enjoyed those kinds of engagements because they weren't as stressful as preaching to adults.

I was invited to speak to the youth where a couple of my peers attended. Before going to that service, God had instructed me to preach about Jeremiah, the prophet called at a young age. God also told me He was going to show me a couple of people He'd chosen for ministry. That day, the church was full of young people and adults. I gave the word and encouraged the young and the old by telling them that God wasn't concerned with their age. While ministering the word, God revealed who He had chosen to be vessels for His service. During the call for salvation, I also started a line for those who wanted prayer. I called for those who had been selected by God to come to the front. One of the gentlemen chosen was already scheduled to preach his trial sermon the very next Sunday. What an amazing confirmation from the Lord that he was doing the right thing.

The next two chosen vessels were my peers. Back in the day, we all served as musicians for our church. Neither one of them prepared for what God had to say. They were shocked that God was calling them into ministry. Both were college sophomores, living away from home. They would later tell me that they weren't so sure about preaching the gospel. I reassured them by saying they shouldn't worry because God would eventually reveal His will in such a way; they wouldn't be able to deny it. The presence of God was there to assure those chosen that His hand was definitely upon their lives.

The Lord continued to develop the gifts in my life. I noticed that God would often reveal the gifts and callings of those in the audience of the services I conducted. It was exciting to confirm or disclose the plan of God to them. It was evident that there were a lot of people who needed direction and encouragement. I continued to seek God for more wisdom and revelation of His word to help the body of Christ. The opportunities to share the gospel continued to increase. God is indeed a rewarder of those who diligently seek Him.

As a church, we participated in a yearly celebration for Jesus. I was asked to share, along with another young lady from our church. Churches from various places would come together to celebrate Jesus. This particular year the anniversary celebration was scheduled to take place out of town. I was nervous because this was the first opportunity to speak in another county. I prayed to God for a word to say to these seasoned believers.

Ten minutes was given to each of us to share what was on our hearts. I offered to let my sister go first. She read a remarkable poem about God. As I walked to the podium, fear was gripping me. My words came simply in the form of a testimony. I started by confessing to the congregation that having to stop dancing was a big concern for me once I became a Christian. I gave them the answer God had given to me. The answer was that I didn't need to stop dancing. I could continue to dance; I just had a new partner, the Holy Spirit! Listen, the Holy Spirit immediately covered the room, and of course, I began to dance. Many others started to dance and celebrate Jesus along with me. After the service, an older gentleman in his seventies approached me. He wanted to thank me for sharing my testimony. He confided in me that he had not been able to dance for the Lord in over ten years due to arthritis. He testified that the power of God hit him, and he was ready and able to dance again. I was thankful and amazed by the power of God.

After a year, my Pastor awarded me a missionary license. I continued to spend time with God to sharpen my ear for His voice. I was beginning to experience more dreams and visions. The mantle of prayer became a part of me. I couldn't understand why praying for someone instead of preaching to them felt more fulfilling to me. Praying for others during the altar call was part of my ministry. I set aside time to request that the congregation come forward and pray. God's presence would always fill the room as we poured our hearts out to Him during that time.

One of the mothers asked if I would pray about her upcoming court case. She had solicited prayer from her seasoned peers, but they refused. Their reasoning was not valid. Sometimes our lack of understanding causes us to misjudge a situation. Although I was much younger and lacked experience, I believed God. The mother explained that she had hired a contractor to do some remodeling work at her home. The contractor had filed suit against her for nonpayment. According to the mother, the contractor's accusations were false. I didn't know how to pray or what to pray for in that instance, so I asked God how I should pray. He instructed me to anoint the court document, place it on the floor, walk around it seven times while praying in the spirit. The

Holy Spirit just overshadowed us in the mother's living room. I picked up the document and told her that God wanted her to take it with her to court that following Monday morning. I waited in anticipation for the word of victory in this situation. As soon as she arrived home from court, she called to share her testimony. The judge read the accusations against her and determined that the contractor was not telling the truth. He ruled in the mother's favor, the case against her was dismissed, and resolved as "Paid in full." Hallelujah! The Lord God, strong and mighty, had done the impossible!

I prayed for the sick on many occasions. One of the well-known Pastors in the community was ill in one of the local hospitals. When I arrived to visit with him, he was weak but upbeat. Discharged from the hospital, his wife called, and I came to visit and pray. While standing as we prayed, I saw a clear vision of the Pastor in a light blue casket but could not reveal that it was Pastor's season to die. So, immediately, I began to pray for strength for his family and comfort for our beloved Pastor. The family never knew what I saw, but they were grateful for the prayer. The Pastor passed away a month later.

Every Christmas, my family would travel to their hometown. Before going that year, God gave me a night vision about a Pastor who was sick and Pastored two congregations. In the night vision, he had passed away, and they were traveling with his body in a carriage. His remains were being taken from one church to the other for the final viewing by his parishioners. As they arrived with the Pastor's body, I walked up to the carriage and laid my hands on the casket and prayed. The Lord miraculously touched the dead Pastor, and he rose from the dead. After waking up, I began to pray for the Pastor every day from that point. My great aunt was having a phone conversation with my mom about us coming for our regular Christmas visit. While talking, she revealed that their Bishop had had a stroke, and they were unsure if he would live. Mom shared the information with me; God said that's the person in the vision. He Pastored two different congregations.

Two months later, we arrived a couple of days before the scheduled annual Christmas service. God had touched the Bishop's body, and he was in attendance. Constrained from being exuberant, but he never lost his praise. I greeted him with a hug and asked if I could encourage him. I shared some of the vision with him. I described how I had been shown his death a month before his sickness and how God had resurrected him. The Lord confirmed to Bishop his prayers. God had added years to his life. To see the joy of the Lord on the face of the Bishop as he praised God was a memory, I will never forget.

CHAPTER 5

Learning the Call

Learning the Call

I continued to seek God for more revelation and training. Reading books, praying, and practicing on the drums took up a lot of my time. It was great because I felt like I was obeying God. One day my neighbors invited me to fellowship with them at their church. This ministry literally blew my mind! They were prophetic, and they possessed an unusual musical anointing. The level of gifting among the members was at a level I'd never seen before. Although this church setting was indescribable, I never received instructions to become a member of this organization. I observed as they facilitated the Holy Spirit. In a night vision, the Prophet came to me and stated that God told him I was there for training. God answered my prayers; I was learning how to flow in His presence.

One of the things I noticed right away about this particular organization was that they didn't appear to be afraid to allow God to maneuver how He wanted. Their church schedule, how long they worshipped, and the order of the service was utterly foreign to me. The first night I was there, I cried like two newborn babies! Their worship touched my soul in a way I couldn't explain. The presence of God was like a cloud that sat on top of the service. During my course of study, I had always imagined being in an atmosphere where miracles would happen frequently. This place was everything I had read about in the bible and books. The worshippers moved about in the service without hesitation. It was as if they were programmed and always in place, ready for the move of God. The preaching of the word was dynamic. Most nights, it was preaching as I had never heard. I remember taking notes so I could go back and study to gain a better understanding of what I had just heard.

Another detail about this organization that caught my attention was that everyone seemed to be gifted, even the children. I had never seen so many musicians and singers in one church during a single service. Whenever I went, I would sit in the same area, but never with the same people. It appeared that with every service I attended, someone who I'd seen in the audience at a previous service, was now playing the organ. The next visit, it was the same thing all over again, except there would be a different bass player or drummer. The Pastor/Prophet was an anointed organist and singer. Being a musician myself, I was completely blown away by the sound produced by the musicians and singers. They were very disciplined and never seemed to miss a beat or the instructions given by their leader. I would have gone back just to experience them the music ministry. The anointing was so dominant, and many nights resulted in a new song. The development and execution of these new songs were so smooth, it was impossible, as a visitor, to believe that they had not heard or rehearsed the song sometime before the service. Many nights, I wept like a baby as God ministered to my soul.

The stream of the prophetic, which was operated by this church, enhanced and nourished my own gift. I began to desire more of God than ever before. The remarkable thing about this church was that they had three operations that stood out. They effectively operated in the prophetic, in the working of miracles, and the music ministry. I was drawn to it all like a pupil getting instruction. My prayer had been to understand the prophetic more and to see it in operation. The book of Acts was in full effect in their services.

When God would get ready to release a new song, the weight of the anointing would be overwhelming. The prophetic songs would always start with the Pastor, and the singers would immediately learn their parts and begin to sing. One night the Pastor began to sing a love song. Now, that was unusual to hear in a service that was not a wedding. This organization had designated specific orders of service for friendship and marriage. While singing, the Pastor left the stage and began to walk the aisle. I watched him closely because I couldn't figure out just what he was getting ready to do. He chose a married couple and began to sing the love song to them. The couple started to weep and hold each other tightly. I can't even put into words how beautiful it was to witness the power of God touch people through a love song sung in a church setting. Later that night, the couple testified that they had been discussing divorce. An argument between them had taken place right before the service. They made a conscientious effort to attend the scheduled service, despite their differences. *"Obedience is better than sacrifice" (1 Samuel 15:22 NLT).* They testified later that evening that they would not give up on their marriage. The couple would seek counseling.

The other thing that I liked about the ministry was their belief in evangelism. One night they came to a town located near my home. I can't describe how excited I was to go just a few miles to be part of their service. God's presence filled the service. Revelatory preaching and great singing blessed my soul. I witnessed testimonies of how God would anoint aspiring musicians to start playing like professionals. Well, I saw it for myself, and it was phenomenal! The Prophet simply asked if there was anyone there who would like to play an instrument for the Lord. The host Pastor's son raised his hand and stated that he wanted to play the organ. The Prophet instructed the young man to sit at the organ and play what he could, so the son played a couple of chords. The Prophet asked him, "If I pray for you, will you play for God and keep your gift for the church?"

The young man answered, "Yes. I will." A prayer was prayed by the Prophet, asking God to impart the gift to the young man. The Prophet then began to play a song, and he asked the Pastor's son to play the same song after him. Listen, the son started to play the song, and the entire church went wild! Moments like that will always be dear to my heart. I saw the miraculous happen before my eyes; it gave my faith a boost like nothing I'd ever seen before.

The more I attended their services, the more I began to realize just how important this was for me. Every service was affording me a chance to see God move without restriction. They were always ready and willing to be used by God. They traveled with a team that consisted of seers, prophets, singers, musicians, and deacons. In one of their evangelistic services, the prophet ministered a word and prepared to do an altar call. He did something I'd never seen before. He asked all the ministry gifts, except the musicians, to come and minister to the people. They came from all over the audience while he sat on the steps and watched. Now, this made my head spin! There were at least ten to twelve people sharing words of knowledge, laying hands, and administering deliverance. The Prophet stated that he wanted everyone to know that God wants to use everyone, not just the senior leaders. If I had to name that experience, it would have been called the School of the Spirit.

The experience was incredible and has stayed with me. It was like going to see a movie, but you are in the film, watching every scene. I'm so appreciative of God for allowing me to spend those few years observing and being in the midst. I was excited, and my faith grew by leaps and bounds. I continued to visit that ministry for the next couple of years. I realized that what I had witnessed would probably never be part of my circle. Accepting the hard truth was disheartening. I knew that God didn't favor congregations over each other.

The choir was the closest experience I'd encountered, where I was able to witness God move without limitations. Many of us developed dear friendships, and some even found their spouse while participating in the choir. The Love Fellowship Choir had ministered non-stop for five years. Many of the members moved away, got married, or became employed. Our numbers decreased drastically, and we began to limit our ministry to the local area. Watching the Holy Spirit move over the audience while we ministered, people accepting Jesus, and healings created memories that shaped my ministry. My Father in the Lord was a prayer warrior! Watching him minister to people gave me great insight. The prophetic often counseled him as he prayed for others.

CHAPTER 6

The Fall

The Fall

While participating in the choir, a lot of us became friends. We spent a great deal of time together at family cookouts, church services, traveling, and just having a good time together. There were a lot of unforgettable memories created. Time spent with my parents and friends helped me forget the strain I felt while doing ministry. I continued to share God's word locally for youth events.

The battle of trying to prove that God had called me became overwhelming for me. Some in the church believed that God had not called me. They were convinced that I was doing it all for a show. Was it possible for God to speak to me, perform miracles, and reveal dangers? Many didn't believe, and they were jealous of the influence God had given me.

The revelation gifts upon my life created even more chaos. I knew if I continued to remain in prayer consistently, I would gain the will and the strength to obey God at any cost. I contemplated for over a month as to what I could do to make things better for myself. Finally, I concluded that spending less time in prayer would position me to hear God less than usual. My decision would prove to be one of the worst decisions I'd ever made in my life.

As time progressed, I began to resist using the revelation gifts while ministering. This idea seemed to keep down some of the confusion in my life. That took a lot of pressure off me, and I felt like I was finally getting my feet under me. Although I was uncomfortable disobeying God, it just made ministry a little easier.

Slowing down my prayer life and not completing my ministry assignments didn't stop God from revealing knowledge. The word of knowledge and the word of wisdom were still often used by God to show His will for others. I continued to pray His will over the matter until I saw God's results. A few months had gone by, and I was beginning to feel guilty for not seeking God with the same determination and passion I used to have. Spiritually, I started to feel a shift that I'd never felt before. Praying and reading my bible had always been like fuel for me. I never really gave a lot of thought to the possible consequences I could face for the lack of time I spent with God. The Lord not only used dreams and visions to help me pray for others, but He also used them to warn me of danger as well.

One night, in a vision, while sleeping, I saw myself in a lesbian relationship. I was in total shock, and I was positively sure that would never happen to me. Succumbing to that level of temptation was highly unlikely. I went about my daily routine and spent only a few minutes praying about what God had shown me. Pride began to counsel me into believing that was never going to happen to me, and that there wasn't any reason for me to worry. I never discussed what I had seen in that vision with anybody, and I eventually placed it in the back of my thoughts. As time progressed, I began to feel as if I was internalizing feelings that God had shown me in the vision. I continued to convince myself that I was just going through a phase. Praying to God about it seemed to be irrelevant. After all, there was no way this was going to happen!

In times past, whenever God had revealed danger for others to me, He gave instructions for victory. I wasn't exempt. A couple of months went by, and just like God revealed, I found myself involved in a lesbian relationship. I couldn't believe it was happening. How could I have been so careless? God warned me, and I denied that it could happen. I repented to God and began asking Him to wash my mind and soul. I eventually started to walk in shame and guilt. There was also a younger preacher who often ministered to the choir. He shared with me his struggle to remain celibate for the Lord and asked for prayer. I thought this was an excellent time to share my struggle. I believed he was going to pray for me, as well. The next day, my immediate church circle knew all about my relationship. I never revealed his struggle, but shortly after, he stopped preaching.

During my ministry, I was an advocate of God's mercy and His willingness to give you another chance. Somehow, it was different for me because of the type of sin I had committed. I remember how my church circle treated those who became entangled in sexual perversion. I saw the looks and heard the whispers. Many of them suggested that unfriending my friends would be best for me, due to their choices. I never understood why we were throwing them away and not trying to help restore them.

Now, it was time for me to face the people for my choices. I repented to my Pastor and the church. My Pastor told me to come, and if there were a Deacon present, it would be received. The night I confessed my sin, there weren't many in attendance. Some members were angry and said it should have been done during a Sunday service. My Pastor responded that I had done what was required; he sincerely wanted to see me restored. I'll always love him for telling me I could get up again. After seeing the actions of my church circle, I seriously contemplated leaving.

Low self-esteem and shame were like a ball and chain around my ankles. I believed that God still loved me and would restore me. Unfortunately, my church circle struggled to have faith that I could recover and eventually preach again. Well, I made up my mind that going back to church was what my soul needed. Arriving at church late, trying to avoid questions or stares, became a way of life for me. Although I was in a state of needing to be restored, there were some things I could still discern. Homosexuality began to be the sermon text whenever I came to church. It was as if they were trying to use the sermon to fix me. Service after service, the sermon text remained the same. I knew the target was going to be me every time I gathered up enough courage to walk through the church door.

The sad thing was that I never felt the Holy Spirit or the love of God through the messages taught. Knowing that God gives words to help the body of Christ, I couldn't believe that what I was hearing was all He had to say every time I came to church. Church had become predictable and painful for me. My appearance changed the atmosphere, and I was no longer welcome. The sin I committed was an act of sexual perversion. Was my sin more significant than the blood of Jesus?

Leaving the church, and God, looked to be the only thing left to do. I felt as though I had done too much and that it would be best for me to start a new life. I began to go into a dark place of rejection. In my mind, I couldn't get beyond what I had done. I felt that I had caused God too much trouble, and I had embarrassed my parents. There were many days spent in my room alone, after work, so I wouldn't have to meet the eyes of people I knew. I had become the talk of the town! I will always love and have the most profound respect for my parents and how they tried to encourage me. To me, this season seemed like it would never end.

The depression led to intense feelings of suicide. Self-rejection had kicked in, so I felt my life was worthless. There were many days I traveled across a bridge, feeling the intense urge to drive over into the river. Leaving this world seemed so enticing, I couldn't stop the compelling feelings of suicide. One of the strangest things about this stage of my life was that I was still dreaming. I thought to myself, "Lord, you want me to pray for someone else, and I can't even help myself!"

Eventually, I got better because of the prayers of my mother. Her plans for me were to return to church and continue where I had left off. It was very

73

disheartening to tell her I no longer considered myself a Christian. I was willing to give up my first loves, drumming, and preaching, to find out who I really was.

The next few months of my life was a journey I couldn't have imagined. Everything seemed upside down! Sometimes, I would attend church out of town. Part of me wanted to stay connected. God never said He was through with me; I just assumed He was. He was still chasing me and showing me that He had never left me. He even warned me against reconnecting with an old boyfriend in a night vision. Three weeks later, I ran into him while driving along the road. We hadn't seen each other in a couple of years. Conversations began to be a daily thing between us. The next thing I knew, I was sleeping with him. It felt as if we were trying to reconnect and make up for the lost time. Again, I had made the mistake of dismissing what God had revealed to me. Deep down in my heart, I was wondering if I could reconcile with my ex-boyfriend and move forward. Fear convinced me that I would end up getting hurt again; so, I played it safe and said no to a commitment.

After committing adultery, I knew it was over for me. The need to separate myself from my old life was evident. Making good choices was no longer possible for me. This process included getting rid of my church clothes and trading in my truck for a sedan. I wanted nothing in my life to remind me, or others, of the preacher I used to be. Sometimes, I would run into younger adults, and they would say, "Aren't you the preacher who came to our church?" They would also remember how I played drums for their events. It irritated me that they recognized me because I just wanted to be done with the old me and move on to the new me. I lost a lot of friends who were Christians. Some received prophecies and warnings from God through me, but it was now just a thing of the past. I'd become an outcast. This evidence proved I was making the right decision by leaving God and His people.

This transition was going to be interesting because the church was all I knew. Smoking, drinking, and partying was foreign to me, but I was ready to learn how to do it. Now that I was going to have some free time, I enrolled in college, aspiring to be in the criminal justice field. The night courses were appealing because I worked full time during the day. Working and attending college was my only plan. Although I was no longer aligning my life with Christianity, I had no desire to be involved in another relationship. Leaving God left my soul wide open for all sorts of opportunities, though. The conviction I once felt was now a thing of the past. There were no limitations to my choices in life. The one thing I needed to make clear to everyone was that I was no longer a Christian, and my persona had changed entirely.

After experiencing lesbianism, there were past situations I questioned. Motives and actions of other women made me realize that I was running all along. I made decisions because I felt like some friendships were moving in the wrong direction. Some were unhappy, although I was trying to protect our friendship. I realized that in some cases, my friendliness toward people and my loyalty to the people I considered friends created misconceptions. I thought about how I handled friendship was the norm. There was one night I distinctly remember. I attended Bible Study regularly with a friend, and that night I rode with her. As I was getting ready to get out of her car, she leaned over and kissed my cheek. I pulled away quickly because it didn't come from a pure place. It was months before I ever addressed what happened that night. I just wanted to forget that it ever happened.

All kinds of thoughts were flooding my mind. What if I had been in denial about my sexuality my entire life? Why did God allow me to go down this path? Had I ever been called to serve God? The gifts and callings on my life, were they just for a season? Deep down, I still loved God, but I thought He didn't love me anymore, and He no longer had use for me. I dismissed facts that God was able to forgive and restore my soul.

CHAPTER 7

New Life

New Life

Entering a new phase in my life was exciting. To say that things had never been this way before for me was an understatement. The first thing I came to appreciate and enjoy about my new lifestyle was not having to go to church. Not having to see people whispering and making remarks from the pulpit felt so good. I wondered why I stayed so long. It was a waste of my time; that life was over. In my heart, I'd begun to force myself to believe that God no longer loved me, especially now. This decision was vital. It meant that I would not be labeled a hypocrite. Leaving was the mature thing to do. My heart wanted to change, but my soul was warring.

Looking for a new relationship wasn't on my list. I needed time to come to terms with my life. So, I was content with being single, trying to figure out who I was. The older saints used to say the first thing a backslidden preacher will do is begin to curse. Now, that was on point for me. The profane words seemed to roll off my lips. It was as if I'd been cursing all my life. One of my funniest memories happened when my mom pushed the button that controlled the windows in our car, as the window started coming up, it squeezed my hand. Pain shot up my arm like lightning. Oh, my goodness, I said, "Oh, sh*t!"

The words came out before I knew it! I looked at my mom, convicted and embarrassed at the same time. She said, "Baby, I'm so sorry about your finger." She laughed and never mentioned that I'd cursed. Mom always knew when to chastise and when to lighten the moment. The truth of the matter is that she loved me so much, and because I was acutely aware of her love for me, the conviction was always present when we were together. I made a point of not using profanity in her presence, but the rest of the world was not exempt.

There was a great deal of time on my hands, and I had no clue about what to do with it. It seemed as if the only thing I had to do was live, love my parents, and work. Imagine me thinking that I didn't need God to do that. Gradually, I was getting comfortable being away from the church.

While I had so much time on my hands, I put my plan to attend college into action. I enrolled in the Criminology program and began my night courses. I continued to work during the day, relieved to have very little time to think about my past. Starting over can be filled with uncertainty, but I was determined to live without the church. There were so many things that I still didn't understand about sexual perversion. One night while attending one of my college classes, I walked by a room filled with students. The door was open, and I saw a female student watching everyone passing. I never saw her on campus again, but I continued in my classwork for the next year, then graduated.

After graduating, a new position became available on my job. Management would be selecting employees from within the store, as well as new employees. I applied for the position, was accepted along with several others. Spending time with my parents and working was my new life, so I welcomed the change in my routine.

While leaving work one day, the new hires were standing near the time clock. I gave the whole group a quick glance, then took a double take. To my surprise, the female student from the college class was in the group. What were the odds of me seeing her here? The new employees worked in different areas. Occasionally, I saw her during our morning break or leaving with her boyfriend. One day after our shift ended, she asked me for a ride home. I took her home, and we exchanged numbers. Slowly, over time, we became friends, and we started carpooling to work. I wondered what happened to her boyfriend. When I asked her, she told me that nothing had happened to him and that they were still friends. We started spending a great deal of time together, and I eventually met her family. By that time, I was aware that there was definitely a level of attraction between us. My mind told me to run for my life. The last time something like that happened to me, it had ended in chaos.

With all this going on, I encountered an old friend. A few years back, our friendship became strained because I felt we were going in the wrong direction. I was convicted and felt the need to be responsible for maintaining a healthy bond between us. During a visit here, she and her friends want to visit a park for the weekend. I didn't see any harm in that, and I was grateful for the opportunity to getaway. Later that night, she began to express her feeling about me from years back. We had never discussed any feelings. You could not have prepared me for this conversation.

Thinking about what she said, I knew I also had unresolved feelings for her from years ago. After a week, we continued to communicate. I decided to visit her and bring closure to what we'd discussed. Now, I knew that it was a chance that I had a potential new relationship forming. In my mind, I was single. That meant there were potential relationships around every corner. My pride told me I could do anything I wanted to do, even though my old friend was married. I convinced myself it was okay because we wouldn't continue to see each other. With little consideration of how I might be breaking the heart of my potential new friend, I made plans to visit. We would be safe because this was only for the weekend. There was to be no continuation; this was the first, and the last time we'd act on our mutual feelings. No matter how much I tried to be firm about my choices, a part of me was feeling somewhat indecisive. I had never just 'planned' to sin. The more I thought about it, the more I was convinced that this was only a "friends with benefits" type situation.

I arrived at my destination, still trying to make sense of how far I'd gone from my beliefs. We were both happy about the visit but somewhat anxious at the same time. Guilt was trying to grab me, to pull me back from my plan. I had been there for a couple of days, and everything seemed to be okay. The husband was nice and treated me well. I refused to believe that conviction was what I was feeling. The connection I once had with

God and the church was disconnected. I should have been able to just flow in my new existence, but my nerves were starting to get the best of me. I pressed pass those feelings as we secretly planned our time together. Monday came; it was finally our moment to be together. At this point, I was absolutely certain that God was done with me because I'd completely given up.

To the best of her knowledge, my friend's husband never came home once he left for work. This day was an exception. We were in the spare bedroom when we heard her husband's keys unlocking the front door. We scrambled to get ourselves together. She rushed out of the room while I pretended to be packing my clothes. Although I no longer considered myself a Christian, I believe God allowed her husband to come home unexpectedly to stop what we had so carefully planned. I often wondered if he ever figured out what was going on between us. The next day, I made plans to leave a day early. I couldn't face her husband, so I came up with an excuse to leave.

Once I got back home, I began to think about what could have happened if we had been discovered together. Violence could have erupted and either, or both, of us, could have been hurt. Not to mention the mental anguish of finding out your wife has a female lover. That would have been a worse scandal than the one I was trying to move past. I was going from bad to worse in a spiraling downfall. But nothing terrible had happened; I made it safely back home.

After arriving home, my potential new girlfriend and I discussed dating and whether or not I thought I was ready for a relationship. The one thing that jumped out to me was that she was unchurched. That meant that neither of us would have a connection to the church. We could do whatever we wanted to do without fear of conviction or condemnation. All these thoughts rolling around in my head led me to one conclusion. Not only had I left the church, but I was also cutting ties with the women in the church. I needed to make a clean sweep of my past affiliations. There would be no straddling the fence. It was still shocking to find out how many Christian women were involved in or were potential candidates for lesbianism. It seemed to be a secret community. Staying away from those types of relationships would distance me from any conviction about my lifestyle. Although this seemed like a great plan, it didn't stop God from reminding me of who I was. One night I had a night vision of my great aunt, who raised me during my childhood years. My great aunt, who was already deceased, appeared dressed in a beautiful white robe with wings. She began to follow me, saying, "stop running from God His hand is upon your life!" I began to run seemingly, five miles, trying to get away from her. The night vision ended with me continuing to run, and never stopping to acknowledge what she was saying.

CHAPTER 8

Settling In

Settling In

Well, after a few days had passed, I said yes to starting a new relationship. Knowing that I could opt-out at any time if it didn't go well made me feel better about everything. I wasn't a player, and I believed in a committed relationship. Although, after analyzing past scenarios, it would have been easy to join the multi-partner game. It puzzled me why women were attracted to me. It appeared that my gift to play drums and preach attracted women who were considered weaker than me. The call of God upon my life caused me to look like a covering. I've learned that no matter what their partner preferences may be, most women are just searching for cover.

Lesbian relationships vary in what roles are played by the individuals. The women who were attracted to me viewed me as a *stud-femme*. I learned later that lesbians weren't defined by the functions, but by their love for each other. Being seen as a stud-femme wasn't something I considered to be a lifetime role for me.

My girlfriend and I never discussed which roles we'd play. Things were going well between us, and I felt I had made the best choice. As we dated, it became apparent that I was a *femme*, and she was a *stud-femme*. It just happened without any odd feelings or adjustments. My appearance was also changing. My wardrobe now consisted of spandex shorts, t-shirts, jeans, and sandals. All church clothes, except for two outfits, were given to Goodwill. I no longer needed them.

For the first time in a long time, I felt free to do what I wanted. There were only two people who concerned me, my parents. What would they think about me living as a lesbian? It was never my intention to dishonor or hurt them with my choices. If I was going to be out late, or not coming home for the night, I would call them so they wouldn't worry. How could I think they wouldn't worry about their child who now professed that she was no longer a Christian? My mom was already laboring in prayer for my dad's soul, and now her baby was in trouble.

At times, it still felt strange to be out in the world because the church used to be my life. I thought the stage of convictions was entirely over. The pride in me said repentance was no longer needed, convinced that this life was what I really wanted. The boundaries began to slowly drop off as I continued to walk away from the Lord. I didn't care if I felt strange during this phase of my life.

My new girlfriend had no idea I was once a preacher. She only knew I once attended church and wasn't interested in it anymore. Starting a relationship, thinking that you may not be in it for long, wasn't right, nor was it fair to her. One night, she and I were talking, and I tried to warn her of a possible abrupt change. My words were, "I know you don't know me, but I don't know how long I'll be doing this. I might just wake up one day and leave the lifestyle." Giving it, some thought later I couldn't believe I said that to her. Why would I do that? Looking back now, I believe the Spirit of God spoke over my life to declare my future as He had planned it. Grace and mercy were keeping me.

Transitioning to a permanent lifestyle change meant there was no longer a need for my truck to carry instruments. Super stoked to have a new vehicle and to use my savings for upgrades. My girlfriend loved it, so that was the icing on the cake. Listen, life was great; a new job position, new girlfriend, new car, and the liberty to do what felt right to me. We continued to bond, spending a great deal of time driving to different cities, just to get away from home. She introduced me to her family. Although our relationship was more than a friendship, it was evident to me that what we had together was strong enough to survive the speculation that always surrounds a lesbian couple.

Dating opened up different types of life. I was naïve to a lot of things done outside of the church. Many of my church friends had disappeared, counseled to stay away from me. There was a lot of time available to get to know my girlfriend and her family and to feel comfortable around them. It was clear that her family loved each other and were very close. Sometimes they disagreed, but they would always seem to make up and be one happy family all over again. My girlfriend was a great help to her family. To see her dedication to her family was a plus for me. Like her, I loved and valued my family.

We were spending a great deal of time together, but intimacy was not at the top of my list. Our relationship was growing, and I was beginning to feel

87

more secure. We took things slow, and it allowed us to develop a friendship before we experienced the next level of commitment. Maybe I was a little hesitant to take our relationship to the next level. Emotionally, it would mean taking a chance. While the dynamics were different from my last encounter, it almost felt like this was too good to be true. After dating a couple of months, I decided I was ready to give it a try.

The role of a femme during intimacy was new to me, but it felt right. I sensed greater sexual fulfillment as a femme. Feeling absorbed in my new relationship, the memories of God and church seemed to be a place I would never return. Although I was still learning about lesbianism, the one thing I was sure of was that intimacy would change our relationship. Secretly, I was hoping that becoming intimate would not cause stress between us. I'd seen how some heterosexual couples get crazy after intimacy. Would it be the same for us?

Next on my agenda was figuring out how to introduce her to my parents. There wasn't an announcement made by me about my sexuality, but most people thought I was continuing to live the lifestyle. It seemed as if my girlfriend's neighborhood, family, and my old associates knew we were a couple. Sharing my choices with my parents was going to be hard because of my love for them. Making them feel as though I was asking them to accept my girlfriend was not my intention. Out of respect, I never announced my new relationship. In my heart, I knew my mom was aware of our lesbian relationship. Initially, it bothered me because I knew she

88

had not given up on the call of God for my life. Mom was the epitome of unconditional love. She disagreed with my choices, but she never made me feel as though I'd gone too far. One day she shocked me asking me to drink at home; so, I wouldn't drive while intoxicated. I was completely thrown off guard by her request. She knew something I didn't know! Her 'prayers' were stronger than my new habit. Well, I started drinking at home, but after about a month, I no longer desired to drink! Now, I believe my mom prayed over that alcohol. I didn't give it much thought, but Mother White resolved that her child was going to be free from these new lifestyle choices. She embraced my girlfriend just like she embraced my friends from church. Her actions kept the conviction of God over my head, and there was nothing I could do about it! Her prayers were more powerful than her words.

At this stage, I was the talk of the town among the churches in my county and adjacent counties. Many questioned if I ever knew God. My decision to not come back to church further validated their beliefs about my past relationship with the Lord. One night an old acquaintance from high school and church wanted to say hello. We met up for dinner to catch up on our lives. I hadn't seen her in a couple of years. To my surprise, she started the conversation off by saying her mom had filled her in on my recent life story. Why was I even shocked to hear this? Everybody else was talking about me; why wouldn't her mother talk about me too? My friend completely stuns me again by admitting her interest in me during high school. I was amazed by her candidness.

The fact that I had a girlfriend didn't bother her one bit. She would settle on flying in to meet me at an undisclosed location. Ultimately, we decided not to follow through with the possibility of a secret relationship. Bitterness and an unforgiving heart were growing like wildfire in me. Just the thought of a person discussing me while their child is trying to sleep with me was crazy! My mind started to think about how many other women were regular church attendees but secretly practiced lesbianism. I was aware that my acquaintance was an avid churchgoer and professed Christian. So, maybe there were lesbians who attended church without any conviction. Although I didn't know the answer right then, I would find out later.

A whole year had almost gone by since I left the church, but the wounds remained. I talked with a friend and shared that I'd left the church. She was utterly shocked by my decision to give up everything. She invited me to get out of the city and spend a few days with her. I told my girlfriend I was going away for a few days. I reassured her that this was just a trip to get away.

When I arrived at my friend's house, it was just strange. There were other women there that I didn't know. As the night went on, they seemed to have an issue with me, but they were churchgoers. So, was it that I was the backslidden person in the bunch? When I couldn't take the passive aggression any longer, I told my friend, "I'm leaving this bullsh*t! I don't have the time nor the energy, and my gun is in the glove compartment".

My friend begged me not to leave, and she offered a solution. These ladies were lesbians, and they were unsure about my intentions. Now, I was ultimately in disbelief that these ladies were jealous. It felt like I was going to have to fight them. I told my friend that I didn't give a d*mn about them singing or preaching in church. In my eyes, they were hypocrites. They seemed comfortable practicing lesbianism and content with their current lifestyle. I knew the difference between trying and settling. It angered me that they were so hostile to me when their souls needed as much help as mine. I was proud to say I wasn't trying to fool God or people. I wanted people to know I was no longer a Christian.

Arriving home, away from all that drama, felt good. As soon as I checked on my parents, I went to see my girlfriend. Immediately, she started questioning me about the trip. I explained everything to her in detail. After all, nothing had happened, and I had nothing to hide. Still, I could tell that she had reservations about what happened those couple of days while I was away from her. Trust issues began to surface. She was angry, and I left thinking we were in trouble. We'd never disagreed before, so this was new to me. After a few days, we talked about what happened again. We concluded that we both had overreacted. Our relationship grew stronger and stronger. I knew that we had fallen in love, so we'd soon get over the trust issue.

Now and then, I'd run into someone from church. They'd ask when I was coming back to church. Most of them were not sincere. They must have thought I'd forgotten that they were part of the crew who continued to reject me, even after I repented before the church. My interactions with them weren't much at all because I knew they didn't care. They had assigned me to hell, and there had been no restoration available for me. There were a few people from the church who showed me the kind of love they were always talking about extending toward the fallen. Those few were concerned for my soul. Whenever I saw them, they never asked about my return to church, but I knew they were praying for me.

There was one church lady who was well known for holding people hostage to their sins, especially the act of sexual perversion. When I say she never forgot, I mean she NEVER forgot! It didn't matter if you moved on in life; she was going to keep your sins before you and before other people. I'd watched her treat people like this before, but who knew I would become a victim of her belief system.

One day she asked when I was coming back to church. I politely stated that I wasn't sure. She repeated the question as if my answer wasn't good enough. Well, I snapped and told her not to ask me about coming back to church ever again. I said to her that I might never come back. By that time, I was angry. She was part of the crew that didn't care. This time, I didn't forget her sin.

Disconnected from the church scene, I remained a hot topic. There was an annual church celebration that I use to attend. When we traveled to these events, we often stayed with friends who were part of the same fellowship. This particular year the event was held locally. A good friend asked if she could stay with me while attending the celebration. A mutual acquaintance of ours tried to discourage her from staying with me. They treated me like an epidemic. Her leaders also discussed my lifestyle with others as they traveled. I applauded my friend for following through with her plans. The gossipers were not aware of our conversation before the celebration. I gave her the option to change her plans because I knew scrutiny would be a weapon against her.

The decision to disconnected from all church services included preaching on the radio and television. The rebellion was at an all-time high in my life. Cursing, sexing, and bitterness was now part of my personality. That was a bunch of stuff going on compared to who I used to be. I was often the target of gossip and competition. The old me never really tried to defend who I was. Those were battles I'd left behind, and I was glad.

There was one friend who always asked me to attend church with him. I had no desire to attend anybody's church; that season had ended a while back. He was so persistent; I couldn't get rid of him. I knew he sincerely loved me and was concerned about my soul. So, to get him off my back, I decided to attend a Sunday morning service with him. I had no idea of the plan God was getting ready to unfold. They had an out of town Prophet as the guest speaker that Sunday. I was hoping the Prophet wouldn't speak to or notice me. He began to minister prophetically after the sermon. He walked up and down the aisles, from the front to the back of the church. I made sure not to even look at the Prophet. A sigh of relief escaped my throat as he walked to the pulpit, signaling completion. Suddenly, he looked in my direction, pointed, and said, "Ma'am!"

I acted as if the Prophet wasn't talking to me. I didn't budge, not even a little bit. Finally, he described what I was wearing. At that point, I knew God had set me up. The Prophet asked me to stand while asking the congregants to point their hands toward me. He said, "Young lady, you are not doing what God called you to do!" He concluded with, "One day you are going to wake up and do what God called you to do. Now, everyone else says power!" Before they could get the whole word out of their mouths, everything went black.

A few minutes later, laid out on the floor, tears streaming from the corners of my eyes, down into my ears and my hair. Although I was in rebellion, I knew that God had spoken a word, and the power of His love had broken through my wall. There were two Apostles, who I knew, seated two rows behind me. While I was struggling to get myself together, I heard one of them say, "Yes, God!" They were in total agreement with the revelation that I needed to allow God to heal my pain so I could begin to obey Him again.

CHAPTER 9

Betrayal

Betrayal

While enjoying my relationship, I was determined to prove I didn't need the church. Sometimes I would think of how quickly they gave up on me; I'd get mad all over again. The only thing that bothered me about leaving God and the church was the knowledge of how deeply I would be hurting and disappointing my mother. I completely stopped talking to God because I thought He didn't want to talk to me. In hindsight, I never heard God say He no longer wanted to speak to me. I just assumed He wouldn't. Thinking about all this would make me feel somewhat unsettled about the choices I was making.

My girlfriend and I started spending more time together out of town. It seemed to feel good not to be in our city. There was a lot of money spent to fund those weekends away from home. After much discussion, we concluded that moving in together would be a great idea. Apartment hunting, saving money, and shopping for furniture was the plan for the next three months. My most significant challenge was to speak to my parents about my plans to move out of their home. The thought of being on my own for the first time brought a mixture of excitement and apprehension. Ultimately, moving in with my girlfriend would confirm any speculations, my parents, friends, and former church associates may have had about our relationship.

We began to search for an apartment and quickly found one. The furniture was paid, so all we needed to do was pay the deposit and move in. Up until this point, our relationship was going well. Suddenly, overnight, we started to argue about little things. It appeared that trust was becoming an issue again. There were days we wouldn't talk to gather our thoughts about the upcoming move. The closer we got to our move-in date, the more things began to escalate. Our arguments got louder, more hurtful, and more frequent. We'd break up and makeup almost daily.

One evening, while in a heated argument, I drove down a secluded road. Our voices were intense with fiery aggression; my girlfriend never noticed I was gripping the steering wheel with all my strength. I was so angry and just sick and tired of going back and forth. After I had driven over a mile down the road, I slammed the car into park. I managed to reach under the seat for my gun. She was still shouting, making accusations. I stepped out of the car and shot the revolver across the field. My girlfriend's voice was taken over by a powerful voice that said, "Kill your girlfriend and commit suicide. No one will find you for a few days". I was so angry until I thought I was willing to go through with it. All the anger in me came rushing towards my trigger finger.

"Pull the trigger!" shouted the anger caused by the way the church treated me.

"Pull the trigger!" shouted the anger caused when my friends turned their backs on me.

"Kill yourself!" shouted the anger caused by the people who made sure my sins were always in front of me.

"Kill her!" shouted the anger caused by my girlfriend's constant accusations. My finger trembled with the weight of all that anger.

Then I heard a more POWERFUL voice say, *"Your mother doesn't deserve to go through the pain of your actions."* That voice continued to counsel me by telling me, *"Your mother will have a broken heart for the rest of her life."* I hadn't heard the voice of God in a long time, but I recognized it immediately. He knew I was troubled about my life at that point. I was no longer happy, but the soul tie kept me from leaving. I needed a reason not to shoot my girlfriend and commit suicide. The love I had for my mother was just enough to cause me to change my mind. I lowered the gun to my side and walked back to the car. God spoke to me, and I listened. My girlfriend asked me why I shot the gun. I told her I was furious, and I needed to do something to let off some steam. I never shared with her my moment of temptation to harm both of us. The trip home was completely silent, never discussing what occurred. God was still speaking to me. I had listened.

"My sheep recognize my voice, and I know them, and they follow me. I give them eternal life and they shall never perish. No one shall snatch them away from me." John 10: 27-28 (TLB).

The whole idea of living together was changed. Maybe we just weren't as happy as we thought we were. I was glad I hadn't spoken to my parents about the move. The pride in me didn't, for one moment, want to give the impression that my choices weren't working out.

While trying to make things better between us, my girlfriend and I started hanging out with an old friend of mine. She seemed comfortable being around my friend, and the three of us even vacationed together. After two years in a lesbian relationship, I could finally accept me.

A few months went by, then out of nowhere, my girlfriend tells me that she feels that my friend likes me. Devastated by her confession, I could only respond with, "Are you kidding me!" I defended my relationship with my friend and denied my girlfriend's accusations. My mind said, "Here we go again with those same trust issues." As time went by, I began to feel that the Lord was calling me back to Him. The gift of the Seer was coming back to me, just as if it had never left me. I began praying for God's will as He revealed it in dreams and visions. I submitted to prayer, but not to a surrendered life. I ignored my feelings and convinced myself that everything was okay. Dealing with the church crew I left wasn't in my plans.

Mom and I made plans to visit my family up north for two weeks. God was doing something behind the scenes that I couldn't articulate. It was good for me to get away from the stress of everything and just enjoy being with my family. As I prepared to leave, I couldn't shake the conversation I'd had with my girlfriend about my friend's feelings for me. I couldn't understand why my girlfriend felt that way. I said my goodbyes and promised to call while gone. Mom and I were very excited to love, laugh, and relax.

A few days passed, and I called my girlfriend to see how she was doing. The conversation was okay, but there was still some uncertainty. I also called my friend to check on her. The call was about to end when she says, "I want to talk to you when you return."

One of the best things about visiting up north was the food choices. There is no better place to get a sub or Chinese food. My family was so excited to see us, and they took us out frequently. It would always feel like a mini-reunion of my great uncle's children, along with my mom and me. We were having such a great time; those two weeks, I felt such relief from the stress of my life back home. There wasn't any arguing, and no hanging up the phone and then making up just to start the cycle over. I started thinking that I needed to make some changes. That was easier said than done. It was evident that my soul was tired, and although it would have been better for my girlfriend and me to part, I just wasn't strong enough to move in that direction.

When I returned, I didn't make immediate plans to see my girlfriend. We had a brief phone conversation, and I decided to see her the next day. While on the phone, she said I sounded different. I had no idea what she meant. When I asked her what was different, she pointed out that our conversation had contained less cursing. I thought the way I expressed myself flowed and sounded the same. Although it had been a couple of years in the past, I believe my girlfriend never forgot that I had once said that I might wake up one morning and decide that I didn't want to live the lesbian lifestyle anymore. Maybe she was sensing that something was happening.

There were a couple of things that I'd been secretly doing. Whenever I was alone in my car, I would listen to gospel music and a little preaching on the radio. God was drawing me back to Him. He hadn't left me; I chose to leave Him. It was apparent to my girlfriend that something about me was changing. I think that frightened her.

I was slowly getting back into the swing of my everyday life. I met up with my friend to do her hair. There was no awkwardness between us or pretense from either of us. In the middle of our laughing and talking, she proceeded to tell me that she realized she had feelings for me. I was left shockingly speechless for a moment. That was the first time there had ever been an awkward silence between us. As soon as I could speak, I told her that what she was feeling wasn't real. Experience tried to convince her she was going through a phase and that everything was going to be alright. Her answer was she was sure her feelings were real and that she had felt that way about me for a while, but she didn't know how to tell me.

Immediately, I started trying to recall anything I had done to initiate her interest in me. Nothing came to mind. She did confirm that I had done nothing to encourage her feelings; I'd only been her friend. Even though I had turned away from God, I didn't want anyone to become entangled in lesbianism. The truth of the matter was it wouldn't be an easy thing for me to walk away from my friend. I felt the need to distance myself from her because I didn't want her to continue the path she was on. I could feel that heaviness in my heart again. She was only a friend, and somehow my choices had enticed her. I was devastated; nothing could have prepared me for her confession.

I concluded that my girlfriend had been right all along about my friend's interest in me as something more than a friend. But how did she know? Somehow, she had seen something I missed. How could I have missed it? After thinking about it for days, I chose to tell my girlfriend about the conversation I'd had with my friend. I thought I was making the best decision. I wanted to show her that I didn't have anything to hide, and she could trust me. She said she was okay with knowing I had no interest in my friend. Convinced that my friend was interested in me, she finally agreed that we could remain friends.

No matter what she said, revealing my friend's feelings made things worse for me. My girlfriend suspected that I was lying about my feelings for my friend. She believed I was cheating with my friend. I was getting tired of the whole thing. But, I wasn't tired enough to surrender my life to the Lord.

One day I received a call from a friend who wanted to share something with me. She was a mutual friend of myself and my friend, who recently confessed that she had feelings for me. I had no clue what she wanted to discuss, but previous experience with friends who had a confession to make hadn't gone so well. The sinking feeling in the pit of my stomach told me that this time was no different.

That sinking feeling was justified. My heart ached while I heard that my friend and my girlfriend were sleeping together behind my back. My friend's conscience was getting the best of her. She told our mutual friend where and when she was meeting my girlfriend. Our mutual friend said she couldn't keep their intimate relationship from me any longer. She revealed dates, places, and times to me. I couldn't believe what I was hearing. My question was, "Why?" Although I was hurt, I was glad I wasn't being taken advantage of anymore. I didn't know how to feel; these were two people I trusted and had given resources to when there were no other options. After about two hours of getting myself together, I confronted my girlfriend over the phone. She denied everything until I began to give specific dates and times.

I ended the relationship feeling like a fool. I didn't want my parents to see that I was a mess. I felt as if I was the subject of a Jerry Springer episode. Two days later, my friend dropped a letter to the house for me. She began to explain how she became involved and the reason behind her choices. Their reasoning made no sense to me. The decisions made by the two of them were selfish, in my opinion. I was crushed by their logic, not knowing how to recover.

With my love-life in shambles, my body became ill. My lungs filled with bronchitis and breathing was a real challenge. I was ordered by my doctor to remain home for a week to recover. My then ex-girlfriend had been visiting regularly, trying hard to reconcile with me. I was too wounded to even think about reconciliation. I just wanted my heart and my body to heal so I could move on with my life. The meds the doctor prescribed for me wasn't effectively clearing the infection in my lungs. Late one night, I was waiting for my aunt to arrive. When she rang the doorbell, I realized I didn't even have the strength to walk to the door. I crawled across the floor and managed to pull myself up to unlock the door. I immediately fell into my aunt's arms. She frantically woke my parents and to the ER we went. Bloodwork ordered to determine if I had suffered a stroke or if I were suffering from some other life-threatening condition. Something was preventing me from walking. Four hours had gone by, and the bloodwork came back normal.

I wasn't allowed to leave the hospital without having gained the mobility in my legs. The doctors, still trying to put a name to what was wrong with me, scheduled me to have an MRI a couple of days later, which was on a Monday. Since I was resting comfortably, I sent my parents and aunt home to get some rest. At that point, I was entirely in the dark about what was going on with my body. My family kissed me goodnight and headed home with the reassurance that they would be back to check on me early the next morning. After they left, I was wheeled into the hospital hallway to wait for a room. As I laid there alone in the hospital bed, the last four years of my life were flashing before me. Tears were streaming down my face because I felt like I had completely lost control of my life. The truth about my ex-girlfriend and my good friend's intimate relationship devastated me. Now, I'm fighting a respiratory illness, and then not being able to walk was all too much for me.

The doctor puzzled by my condition, but he vowed to find out what caused my legs to stop working. Depression was trying to overtake me again. With tears streaming down my face, God began to speak to me. As clear as a bell, I heard God say, *"I love you! Come home; the enemy wants to kill you in your sins. There's nothing physically wrong with you. What's wrong with you will not show up in the test results. Your problem is sin. I allowed the enemy to touch your flesh to humble you. Your pride kept you from being open to my voice."*

My response was, "God, I've done too much. I don't think I can live the life I used to live anymore".

God told me to bring the sexing, cursing, bitterness, and my unforgiving heart to Him. He assured me that He could handle it. I felt God's presence there in the hallway, and His love covered me. I had not prayed in the spirit for a long time. The Holy Spirit began to make intercession for me, and I agreed to bring all my baggage and lay it at His feet. A few days later, the MRI test and everything was completely normal. Tuesday morning, God healed my legs. I attempted to get up and walk to the restroom. The Lord had honored His word, and I was released to go home that Thursday. God is ever faithful.

CHAPTER 10

Restoration

Restoration

***Create a pure heart in me, O God, and put a new and
loyal spirit in me. Psalm 51:10 (GNT)***

What a rough month! I couldn't believe everything I
had gone through!

The doctor placed me on a two-week leave of
absence from work. I needed time for my respiratory
system to recover from my bout with bronchitis.
Spending time with my parents while my health
improved was just right for me. I'd been spending so
much time away from home, and I hadn't realized how
much I missed them. My girlfriend was visiting me as
well, trying to mend our relationship. I was determined
not to reconcile, even though I loved her. It felt as if there
was a war going on for my will. My conversation with
God also weighed heavily on my mind. Trapped, I began
to pray and ask God for help. There was no more
shutting Him out, but it seemed as if my life and habits
weren't changing. Slowly, I started considering giving the
relationship with my girlfriend another chance. The soul-
tie between us began to scream louder than the pain our
relationship caused. The feeling of being betrayed, and
played like a fool, was immense. Losing two people I
cared about at one time was devastating to me.

Gradually, I started spending time with my girlfriend
again. Trust was still a significant issue for me. Was I

ever going to be comfortable with her? Would I ever believe she loved me again? It was awkward; trying to go back to a place of happiness just seemed out of reach. Every time I made up my mind, it wasn't working for me, my soul ached. Little did I know, but God had a plan to help me. God's idea for redemption is always usually a far cry from our method of recovery.

During my early years of preaching, I'd always heard people make claims of what God wouldn't do. One of those claims was that God wouldn't come in an unclean place. The belief was that if a person were in sin, God would not come in the midst. However, God was on a mission to show me He was higher than what my circle preached. One evening, while spending time together, I could feel the war over my soul. Intimacy between us was no longer fulfilling, and I was functioning broken. God showed up to help me do what I couldn't do alone; I didn't have the strength to walk away from this relationship and continue the process of restoration. God works the unthinkable in our lives.

As we embraced, she stepped away and said, "I can no longer do this. I smell the praying oil they use in church, on your neck!" Stunned, I wiped my neck, and there was no evidence of any substance on my neck. It didn't matter. My girlfriend smelled the oil and wanted no parts of our relationship. God had done what He promised to do for me. What I didn't have the strength to do, He did for me. He allowed a supernatural occurrence to happen. God's love for me provided a way of escape.

Days went by, and part of me was relieved, but I didn't know what the next step was. I shared with my mom that I had redirected my life back to the Lord. I made it very clear to her that preaching was something of the past, and I never wanted to do it again. Salvation was all I wanted. In my heart, I wanted my spiritual father to place his hands on me and pray. My mom told me about a singing program at church. I hadn't been to church in years. I had mixed emotions about how people would feel seeing me there. I pushed all that aside and decided my life was more important than the opinions of the church circle. So, I made plans to go to the singing program.

My closet only consisted of two suits that would be considered appropriate for church. I chose the tan suit, got it together emotionally, and prepared for church. While driving, only a half-mile from the church, another driver didn't yield to the oncoming traffic. I hit her, totaling her vehicle. My car spun around in the road and ended up just inches from a cement light-pole.

I sincerely believe the enemy was trying to kill me before I could get to the church. An angel of the Lord dispatched to keep my car from plowing into that cement pole. If I had hit the pole, it would have fallen and crushed the driver's side of my car. Once the gravity of my situation hit me, I began to cry and thank God. I could have lost my life in that split second.

The driver of the other car blamed me for the accident. Thank God other witnesses were honest, and they reported to the police on the scene that I had a green light, which meant the other driver was supposed to yield the right-of-way to me. A friend saw me on the side of the road. She went to my home and brought my parents to the scene of the accident. They wanted me to attend church another time. Mom wanted me to go home and relax. She knew I had experienced a horrible event, and she was concerned that an injury had taken place. I begged my parents to let me go to church. I knew if I could just make it to the altar, I would be alright. They finally agreed to let me go to the service. I'm not sure there's anything they could have said or done that would have convinced me not to go.

During the altar call, I walked to the front of the church with tears streaming down my face. I expressed that I wanted to give my life back to God. My spiritual father prayed for me, fervently. Right then, everything shifted for me.

My spiritual father asked me to be his drummer. I instantly declined. I was struggling to clear my mind of thoughts and desires. I also knew to have me as his drummer would cause an uproar and put him in harm's way. He reassured me that God had instructed him to ask. I needed to yield and say yes to God. Every area of my broken life would be set free. It was a good feeling to be in the company of someone who believed they were bigger than my problems.

With the support of my mom and my spiritual father, I started attending church regularly. The first thing I asked God to do was to help me deal with the people. Alone, I would never be able to handle their stares, their whispers, the snide comments, their unbelief in my restoration, and not wanting me to attend church. But, if God would go with me, I knew I would be able to endure everything thrown at me.

I remember my first Sunday back in church. I played a few songs, and the presence of God overwhelmed me. I was sobbing uncontrollably while my spirit was making intercession. It felt as if God was stripping my soul and ministering directly to all the broken places in me. I heard my spiritual father say, "She's okay. God is healing and restoring her." Many Sundays followed that pattern. Finally, I figured out that God was using the gift of drumming as a tool to usher me into His presence.

I became stronger, but I had a lot of time on my hands. I no longer had the company of my girlfriend to fill those hours after I got off from work. Once again, God had a plan of action for me. An old church friend of mine started inviting me to spend time with her and her husband. I believed she was aware of my past lifestyle, but she wasn't concerned about that. She was on a mission from God to be a safe place for me, outside of my home. My parents loved her, and they greatly appreciated what she was doing for me.

I was concerned about her reputation, but she was only worried that I knew she was my friend. There were days I felt as if I wasn't going to get through the process. So many times, I just wanted to give up. Whenever I had those types of days, I could call or visit her. Her voice would always give me the courage to hang in there. I will be forever grateful to her for the love and kindness shown to me during that time of my life.

My parents were delighted that I had dedicated my life back to God. The last birthday before my rededication, my dad said, "Shot, I'm going to buy you a dress for church." I chuckle now, just thinking about the 'dress for church' idea. Dad didn't know the church lingo, but he knew his baby wasn't the same person she had been. He said it the best way he knew how. He just wanted to encourage me to go back to church.

The process took about a year for me not to feel the pain of being broken. Forgiving seemed to be my hardest struggle. In my mind, I didn't see how I would be able to forgive my ex-girlfriend or my friend. I remember attending a service after the breakup. A well-respected Apostle approached me after the service and began to encourage me. He said God wanted me to forgive and to drop my planned revenge. Shocked, all I could do is accept the word of the Lord. The Apostle had no idea of the torment I was experiencing. He added that God was going to heal my heart from the pain of the betrayal. He said the Lord was calling me back home. Tears streamed down my face once again, conviction covered me, and I knew I had to obey. I continued my process of becoming healed. My heart was feeling stronger, and life was getting better. I surrendered my unforgiving heart towards my ex-girlfriend and my friend. The betrayal had saved my life. It had been a long time since I'd felt such peace and the assurance that God was with me.

Although, in the eyes of some, I would always be guilty of my past sins. I am so happy the blood of Jesus reaches where others can't go. It even reaches to where others don't care to go. I had many questions that were unanswered before I decided to leave God. Since being restored, He has answered all my questions.

My first question was why I had to experience that challenge. It wasn't that I felt I was too good to go through hardships; it was just that those hardships took me so far from who I thought I was. The Lord allowed me to watch a news program after I'd been out late one night. I never forgot that moment. I didn't realize the significance of the show at the time I watched it.

While sitting watching television, the newscaster reported a case study on one hundred gay men, and he had some exciting and astonishing results. The study concluded that 80% of the men tested displayed the same patterns of growth replicated in their brains. The newscaster reported that the test results confirmed that men could actually be born gay. The church rejected that theory. At that time, I did too. As I continued to watch the broadcast, the Lord began to speak. He stated that the world had had it right all the time. The Lord said, "Because I chose you to be a Levite musician, the enemy wanted you as well."

I paused for a moment to get myself together. The conversation continued. The Lord had explained why so many Levites and others in the arts in the church struggle with homosexuality. Based on what I know now, I couldn't deny what the Lord was saying to me.

113

Although I was born with gifts from the Lord, the enemy had also placed lesbian desires in my soul. Chosen to become a lesbian; I was born that way. He reminded me of the example of how Ishmael, Abram's son, was born wild **(Genesis 16:11-12)**. In those verses, the angel told Isaac, *"Return to your mistress and act as you should, for I will make you into a great nation. Yes, you are pregnant, and your baby will be a son, and you are to name him Ishmael (God hears) because God has heard your woes. This son of yours will be a wild one – free and untamed as a wild ass! He will be against everyone, and everyone will feel the same toward him. But he will live near the rest of his kin"* **(TLB)**. This passage confirms that we can be born with issues in our soul that dictate and influence our choices.

The Lord then reminded me of David, who admitted that he was born a sinner and shaped in iniquity. I am no different. *Psalm 51: 5, states, "I have been evil from the day I was born from the time I was conceived; I have been sinful" (GNT).* He wasn't through yet, *John 9:1, "As Jesus was walking along, he saw a man who had been born blind"(GNT).*

What God was trying to tell me was that I didn't wake up and decide I wanted to be a lesbian. Lucifer planted a seed in my soul to influence my choices, as it related to sexuality. He is very strategic in his attacks against Levites. The Lord said, "I knew you would share the truths about your experience and share my heart." Despite how we may feel about gays, God loves

114

everyone, and there is no greater sin. Sin is sin. There is no hierarchy of sin.

In some cases, the church has mishandled those who identify as LGBT. They have advised families to disconnect from their loved ones. Parents, please love your children even if you do not understand their choices. The prodigal story in **Luke 15:11-24** gives a great blueprint of God's mercy and love. My parent's love never wavered, nor were they ever rude to me. As Christians, we use the words 'love people, hate the sin', but in reality, 'hate people, hate the sin.' Some church's response to sexual identity is much like the military. There is a prevailing unspoken sense of "don't ask, don't tell" as it relates to homosexuality. Who can you turn to without being ostracized? There is a great need for accountability for those seeking help. God is not appalled by feelings or temptations to practice homosexuality. He views it as a chance to sacrifice something that appears to be the law of who we are. Yes, many of us were targets of Lucifer's rage. God fired him from the position of Chief Levite, leaving Lucifer with the thought that no one can ever replace me. But, we the Levites and those in the arts, chosen to be a living sacrifice representing the highest form of worship.

My prayer is that my story will encourage those struggling with homosexuality. Depression and rejection have crippled many. God heard my mother's prayers and unleashed a plan to recover me. The same grace I had once preached came and met me in my sins, proving that God's grace and mercy were so much bigger than my sins and failures. The Blood of Jesus, shed on Calvary, washed away my sins, guilt, and shame. There is power in the Blood! It still works! I am a recipient of God's Love and Sovereign Will. He healed my unforgiving heart and the self-condemnation that overwhelmed me. He helped me forgive myself, and I gained my self-worth again. What I had considered a betrayal, saved my life. I am grateful for God's plan of reconciliation. He never gave up on me, and for that reason, I'll never be ashamed of my testimony. Don't quit! God will never give up on you!

Prayer
Father, I pray for the Levites, my brothers, and sisters who are battling with their sexuality. I ask in the name of your son, Jesus, that you provide courage and hope for them. Heal them where they are hurt and unsure of what to do. Speak to their minds where doubt and fear have paralyzed them. Their lives and assignments in the earth realm are relevant. You created us to worship and offer our bodies as a living sacrifice. Father, thank you so much for going after your lost sheep. You are not satisfied with ninety-nine; You come after the one that's lost. I thank you that nothing or no one can keep us from having access to you. Your arms are always open wide and extending mercy to our brokenness. ***"Let us have confidence, then, and approach God's throne, where there is grace. There we will receive mercy and find grace to help us just when we need it" Hebrews 4:16 (GNT).*** Father, I stand in the gap for churches who

singled out our struggle and laughed at our participation. Please help us to forgive those who caused desertion among family members because of the battle. Regenerate our faith that we may worship You in spirit and truth. We lay everything down at the altar. Wash our hearts, our minds, and our souls. Thank you, God, for helping us process our bodies to a place of a living sacrifice. Your Love is immeasurable and never runs out. For this, I give you praise and honor!

Amen!

Made in the USA
Columbia, SC
15 March 2020